CUTTING EDGE

THIRD EDITION

ELEMENTARY WORKBOOK

T0345763

SARAH CUNNINGHAM PETER MOOR
AND ANTHONY COSGROVE

CONTENTS

Grammar focus 1
be: positive forms

1a Complete the text with the words in the box. You may need to use them more than once.

am   is   are

My name ¹ *is* John. I ² _____ married. My wife ³ _____ from Vietnam and I ⁴ _____ from Australia. Our children ⁵ _____ six and eight years old. They ⁶ _____ Australian and Vietnamese!
My wife and I ⁷ _____ teachers. I ⁸ _____ an English teacher and my wife ⁹ _____ a French teacher. Our jobs ¹⁰ _____ great – and the children in the school ¹¹ _____ very nice.

b 🎧 **1.1 Listen and check.**

2 Complete the questions and answers.

A Mariana Ferreira, Brazil
1 A: What *is her name* _____ ?
2 B: Her *name is Mariana Ferreira* _____ .
3 A: Where *is she from* _____ ?
4 B: She *is from Brazil* _____ .

B David and Sarah Jones, Great Britain
1 A: What _____ ?
2 B: Their _____ .
3 A: Where _____ ?
4 B: They _____ .

C Nicole Anderson, Australia
1 A: What _____ ?
2 B: Her _____ .
3 A: Where _____ ?
4 B: She _____ .

D Kenzo Yamamoto, Japan
1 A: What _____ ?
2 B: His _____ .
3 A: Where _____ ?
4 B: He _____ .

Vocabulary
Countries and nationalities

3 Find 11 more nationalities in the word square.

C	A	U	S	T	R	A	L	I	A	N	D	O
H	A	M	E	S	P	F	I	R	S	S	B	R
I	T	A	L	I	A	N	K	J	L	M	P	S
N	J	A	M	E	R	I	C	A	N	F	O	D
E	A	Z	W	M	N	S	A	M	S	R	L	A
S	P	A	N	I	S	H	C	H	I	U	I	B
E	A	T	X	A	S	C	N	B	R	S	S	K
H	N	V	T	D	U	P	I	R	I	S	H	T
C	E	B	A	B	R	A	Z	I	L	I	A	N
S	S	D	R	T	A	M	E	T	C	A	N	W
P	E	T	A	I	T	S	L	I	Y	N	L	I
V	I	E	T	N	A	M	E	S	E	O	F	G
I	S	A	R	T	S	T	A	H	M	E	E	S

4 Add letters to complete the nationalities.

1 With a Ken _y a n_ father and an Amer _i c a n_ mother, this man is a US politician.
2 This tennis player is Ru _ _ _ _ _ . Her boyfriend is a Spa _ _ _ _ singer.
3 This baseball player is Japa _ _ _ _ and he plays in the USA.
4 This Austr _ _ _ _ _ film star is in lots of Amer _ _ _ _ films.
5 This actor is from Canada and his family is Ir _ _ _ _ , Chi _ _ _ _ _ and Brit _ _ _ _ .
6 This footballer is Braz _ _ _ _ _ _ – and Spa _ _ _ _ _ .
7 This pop star is Viet _ _ _ _ _ _ _ .
8 This model is Pol _ _ _ _ and her full name is Katarzyna Strusińska.

5 Match the descriptions in exercise 4 with the famous people in the box.

....

~~Barack Obama~~   Mỹ Tâm   Anna Kournikova
Ronaldinho   Ichiro Suzuki   Kasia Struss
Nicole Kidman   Keanu Reeves

....

1 _Barack Obama_ _____
2 _____
3 _____
4 _____
5 _____
6 _____
7 _____
8 _____

Pronunciation
Word stress

6 🎧 1.2 Listen and repeat the sentences.

1 She's from Russia. She's Russian.
2 He's from Ireland. He's Irish.
3 They're from Japan. They're Japanese.
4 You're from Italy. You're Italian.
5 I'm from Poland. I'm Polish.
6 We're from Spain. We're Spanish.

7 🎧 1.3 Listen to the nationalities. Write them in the correct place in the table to show their stress.

oO	oOo	Oo	ooO	oOoo
		Polish		Australian

Listen and read

8a 🎧 1.4 Read and listen to the texts about four people from different places.

People from different places

Béatrice Santini

Béatrice Santini is from France. She's 28 years old and she's an actress. She's married; her husband is film director Karol Bolewski. Karol is 56 years old. Their home is in Paris.

Donna Fiorelli

Donna Fiorelli is from New York. She's a taxi driver. She's 45 years old. Is she married? Yes, I am . . . I'm married to my job!

David Mills

'Hello. My name is David Mills. I'm 37 years old and I'm single. I'm a bus driver in London. I'm also a writer: my first book is *Bus Driver on Holiday*.'

Plankton

Allan, Doug, Richard and Kirsty are Plankton . . . four musicians from Aberdeen, in Scotland. Their manager is Betty Booth. Betty is from Edinburgh and she's 25 years old.

Lucas Dos Santos

Hi, I'm Lucas Dos Santos. I'm an English teacher from Salvador in Brazil. I'm 57 years old and I'm married.

b Read the text again and answer the questions.

1 Who is an actress?   *Béatrice Santini*
2 Who is a taxi driver?   _____
3 Who is from France?   _____
4 Who are musicians?   _____
5 Who is an English teacher?   _____
6 Who is from London?   _____
7 Who is from Edinburgh?   _____
8 Who is from Brazil?   _____
9 Who is a bus driver?   _____
10 Who is 45 years old?   _____
11 Who is 56 years old?   _____
12 Who is a writer?   _____

Grammar focus 2
be: positive and negative short forms

9 Choose the correct answers.

1 I *'s* / (*'m*) married.
2 They *aren't* / *isn't* Brazilian.
3 You *'s* / *'re* at work.
4 They *'re* / *'s* from Japan.
5 My brother *'re* / *'s* a student.
6 We *'m not* / *aren't* Polish. We're Russian.
7 My parents *aren't* / *isn't* on holiday.
8 They *'m* / *'re* at work.
9 Sydney *isn't* / *aren't* the capital of Australia. It's Canberra.
10 I *'m not* / *isn't* a tourist.
11 You *aren't* / *isn't* a businessman.
12 We *'re* / *'s* fine, thanks.

10 Make the sentences negative.

1 Edinburgh ~~is~~ *isn't* in England.
2 I'm from Ireland.
3 My mother and father are English.
4 Brazil is a small country.
5 My name is Lana.
6 My sister is married.
7 I'm 15 years old.
8 Philip and Elizabeth are on holiday.

Vocabulary
Jobs

11 Put the letters in the correct order to make jobs. The first letter is underlined.

1 r a c t o   _actor_
2 e r n e n g i e   _____
3 e c l i p o c o i f f e r   _____
4 g r e n i s   _____
5 p o s h s t i t a n s s a   _____
6 a n u m i s i c   _____
7 r a w y e l   _____
8 a l l o b f o t e r   _____
9 a i w t r e   _____
10 u s i s b n e s m a n   _____

Pronunciation
Word stress

12a 🎧 1.5 Listen to the words and count the syllables.

1 footballer   _3_
2 police officer   _5_
3 engineer   ____
4 musician   ____
5 businesswoman   ____
6 doctor   ____

b Listen again and look at the stress. Which one is correct?

1 a foot•baller ✈   b footbal•ler   ___
2 a po•lice officer   ___   b police of•ficer   ___
3 a en•gineer   ___   b engine•er   ___
4 a mu•sician   ___   b musi•cian   ___
5 a busi•nesswoman   ___   b business•woman   ___
6 a doc•tor   ___   b doc•tor   ___

Grammar focus 3
Articles with jobs

13a Complete the sentences with *a/an* and the words in the box.

~~police officer~~   footballer   actor   businesswoman
doctor   singer   businessman   waiter
shop assistant   musician
----

1 She's _a police officer_. She works in the police station.
2 He plays for Manchester United – he's _____ .
3 Javier Bardem is _____ from Spain – he's in the film *Skyfall*.
4 Adele is _____ . Her album *21* is great.
5 Lang Lang is _____ from China. He plays the piano.
6 My cousin is _____ in a supermarket.
7 My brother is _____ in Franco's Pizza Restaurant.
8 He works in the hospital. He's _____ .
9 My mum's _____ and my dad's _____ . They're in Tokyo this week, on business.

b 🎧 1.6 Listen and check.

Grammar focus 4
be: personal questions

14a Complete the questions with the words in the box.

~~name~~   business   married   job
address   number   you   from

1 What's your __*name*__ ?
2 Where are you _____ ?
3 Are you here on _____ ?
4 How old are _____ ?
5 What's your telephone _____ ?
6 Are you _____ ?
7 What's your email _____ ?
8 What's your _____ ?

b 🎧 **1.7 Listen and check. Practise saying the questions.**

15 Write short answers to the questions.

1 **A:** Are you Portuguese?
   B: No, ____*I'm not*____ . I'm Brazilian.
2 **A:** Is James English?
   B: Yes, _____ . He's from Manchester.
3 **A:** Is your address 16 New Street?
   B: No, _____ . It's 26 New Road.
4 **A:** Are you and your friend here on holiday?
   B: No, _____ . We're here on business.
5 **A:** Is Barbara married?
   B: Yes, _____ . Her husband's a doctor.
6 **A:** Are you married?
   B: Yes, _____ . This is my husband, James.
7 **A:** Is Thomas an actor?
   B: No, _____ . He's a musician.
8 **A:** Are Anne and Michael American?
   B: No, _____ . They're from Ireland.
9 **A:** Is Howard your surname?
   B: Yes, _____ . My first name's Tony.
10 **A:** Is Jacqueline a teacher?
   B: No, _____ . She's a student.

16a Look at the information about Au Van Bien and complete the questions.

1   Full name: Au Van Bien
2   Job: Engineer
3   Email address: avb@tlctmail.org
4   Nationality: Vietnamese
5   Age: 32

1 *What's your full* _____ name?
2 _____ job?
3 _____ email address?
4 _____ from?
5 _____ you?

b Write Au Van Bien's answers to the questions in exercise a.

1 *My full name's Au Van Bien.*
2 _____
3 _____
4 _____
5 _____

c 🎧 **1.8 Listen and check.**

Vocabulary
Everyday objects

1a Look at the pictures and add letters to complete the objects.

1 b<u>ottle</u> of w<u>ate</u>r

2 ID c _ rd

3 m _ b _ l _ ph _ n _

4 p _ ck _ t of ch _ w _ ng g _ m

5 c _ m _ r _

6 cr _ d _ t c _ rd

7 d _ ct _ _ n _ ry

8 m _ m _ ry st _ ck

9 w _ ll _ t

10 k _ ys

11 ph _ t _ s

12 c _ _ ns

13 t _ ss _ _ s

14 gl _ ss _ s

15 b _ g

16 w _ tch

b  2.1 Listen to Alf talking about the things in his bag. Tick (✓) the things in exercise a he has.

Pronunciation
Word stress

2 🎧 **2.2 Listen and look at the stress. Which one is correct?**

1	a	camera	✈	b	camera ___
2	a	bottle of water ___		b	bottle of water ___
3	a	glasses ___		b	glasses ___
4	a	ID card ___		b	ID card ___
5	a	chewing gum ___		b	chewing gum ___
6	a	credit card ___		b	credit card ___
7	a	dictionary ___		b	dictionary ___
8	a	memory stick ___		b	memory stick ___
9	a	tissues ___		b	tissues ___
10	a	packet of chewing gum ___			
	b	packet of chewing gum ___			

Grammar focus 1
this/that, these/those; Possessive *'s*

3 Look at the pictures and write *this*, *that*, *these* or *those*.

1 _this_ car   2 _____ shoes

3 _____ boy   4 _____ coat

5 _____ chairs   6 _____ men

4a Choose the correct answers.

1 How much is (*that*)/ *those* watch, please?
2 *This* / *These* is my wife, Anna.
3 Are *this* / *these* your keys?
4 Who are *those* / *that* children?
5 Is *that* / *those* your book? What is it?
6 *Those* / *That* 's a nice camera. Is it new?

b Match questions 1–6 in exercise a with answers a–f.

a It's 75 euros. | 1 |
b No, it's six years old! | |
c Yes, it's my dictionary. | |
d They're my brother's sons. | |
e Hello, Anna, nice to meet you. | |
f Yes, they are. Thank you very much! | |

c 🎧 **2.3 Listen and check.**

5 Write *'s* in the correct place in the sentences.

1 Patrick is Jane*'s* brother.
2 Is that Michael car?
3 It's Tessa birthday on Saturday.
4 What's your mother name?
5 Where's Philip desk?
6 My husband name is Peter.
7 Jo is my sister friend.
8 Carla house is in the centre of Rome.

6 Look at *'s* in these sentences. Is it *is* or possessive *'s*?

1 This is a photo of my brother's
  family.   _possessive 's_
2 My brother's an engineer.   _is_
3 Is this John's watch?   _____
4 John's Australian.   _____
5 Our teacher's here.   _____
6 This is the teacher's bag.   _____
7 My father's brother is a lawyer.   _____
8 He's 55 years old.   _____

Pronunciation
this/that, these/those

7 🎧 **2.4 Listen to the sentences. Do you hear *this*, *that*, *these* or *those*?**

1	_that_	4	_____	7	_____
2	_these_	5	_____	8	_____
3	_____	6	_____		

Grammar focus 2
have got

8a Look at the table and complete the sentences with *'ve got*, *haven't got*, *'s got* or *hasn't got*.

	Pet?	Car?	Computer?
Silvia	yes – dog (Rex)	yes – an Audi	no
Martin and Inge	no	yes – two	yes

1 Silvia ___*'s got*___ a dog. His name's Rex.
2 She _____ a car. It's an Audi.
3 She _____ a computer.
4 Martin and Inge _____ a pet.
5 They _____ two cars.
6 They _____ a computer.

b 🎧 **2.5** Listen and check. Practise saying the sentences.

9a Look at the table in exercise 9a again and complete the questions and short answers.

1 **A:** ___*Has*___ Silvia ___*got*___ a dog?
   B: *Yes, she has* _____ .
2 **A:** _____ she _____ a car?
   B: _____ .
3 **A:** _____ she _____ a computer?
   B: _____ .
4 **A:** _____ Martin and Inge _____ a pet?
   B: _____ .
5 **A:** _____ they _____ a car?
   B: _____ .
6 **A:** _____ they _____ a computer?
   B: _____ .

b 🎧 **2.6** Listen and check. Practise saying the questions and short answers.

Vocabulary
Family

10a Look at the picture and information about the Doyle family and complete the sentences.

Sam Doyle – Brenda's brother
Colin Best – Jane's husband
Brenda Doyle – Joe's wife
Joe Doyle – 'Dad'
Jason Doyle – Jane's brother
Jane Best – Joe and Brenda's daughter
Nora Walker (Nana) – Brenda's mother

1 Joe is Brenda's _husband_ .
2 Jason is Joe's _____ .
3 Brenda is Jason's _____ .
4 Joe is Jane's _____ .
5 Joe and Brenda are Jane's _____ .
6 Colin is Jane's _____ .
7 Jason is Sam's _____ .
8 Jane is Sam's _____ .

b Answer the questions about the Doyle family. Write two sentences for each question.

1 Who is Nora Walker?
   She's Brenda and Sam's mother.
   She's Jane and Jason's grandmother.
2 Who is Jason?
   _____
   _____
3 Who is Sam?
   _____
   _____
4 Who is Brenda?
   _____
   _____
5 Who is Jane?
   _____
   _____
6 Who are Jane and Jason?
   _____
   _____

Listen and read

11a 🎧 **2.7** Read and listen to the text about the Iglesias family.

A famous family

Julio Iglesias is from Spain. He was the world's number 1 Spanish singer in the 1970s and 1980s, with songs like Begin the Beguine. He is now the father of a famous family, with eight children. His wife is a Dutch model called Miranda Rijnsburger. They have five children together.

Julio Iglesias also has three children – two sons and a daughter – from his marriage in the 1970s to actress Isabel Preysler, and they are now famous, too.

Julio Iglesias and Isabel Preysler's daughter, Chabeli, is a journalist in Washington. Chabeli's son, Alejandro, and her daughter, Sofia, are young children.

Julio Iglesias's sons are Julio Junior and Enrique. Julio Junior is a model, actor and singer. His songs are in English and Spanish. And his wife is Belgian model Charisse Verhaert.

Enrique Iglesias is also a famous singer. His home is in Miami, Florida, USA. And his girlfriend is Russian tennis star Anna Kournikova. He has a daughter called Leia Rosie.

b Read the text again. Are the statements true (T) or false (F)?

1 Julio Iglesias's wife is called Miranda Rijnsburger. ☐ T
2 Miranda Rijnsburger is a singer. ☐ F
3 Julio Iglesias is Chabeli's father. ☐
4 Isabel is Sofia's cousin. ☐
5 Chabeli lives in the USA. ☐
6 Chabeli is Enrique's mother. ☐
7 Julio Junior is Isabel's brother. ☐
8 Sofia is Enrique's niece. ☐
9 Charisse is Julio Junior's wife. ☐
10 Julio Junior is Sofia's nephew. ☐
11 Chabeli's brothers are Julio Junior and Enrique. ☐
12 Enrique is Russian. ☐

c Put the words in the correct order to make questions.

1 Iglesias / Where / is / Julio / from ?
   Where is Julio Iglesias from?
2 many / he / How / children / got / has ?
   _____
3 is / Alejandro / Who ?
   _____
4 children's / are / What / Isabel's / names ?
   _____
5 job / Chabeli's / is / What ?
   _____
6 wife / Julio / Junior / Has / a / got ?
   _____
7 Is / a / Enrique / singer ?
   _____
8 Where / home / is / Enrique's ?
   _____

d Read the text again and answer the questions in exercise c.

1 *He's from Spain.*
2 _____
3 _____
4 _____
5 _____
6 _____
7 _____
8 _____

Writing
Completing a form

12a Complete the application form with the information in the box.

British   Miss   30/01/2014
c_andon@tlctmail.org

HARLOW SPORTS CLUB

To join HSC, please complete this form.

Personal details

Title: ¹ _____

Surname: *Andon*

First name: *Catherine*

Nationality: ² _____

Date of birth: *18/04/1992*
(dd/mm/yyyy)

Contact details

Address: *3 Green Lane,*
London, SE1 3HH

Email address: ³ _____

Phone (mobile):   *07877 67784*

Phone (home):   *020 7 345 1222*

Signature: *Cmandon*

Date: *(dd/mm/yyyy)*   ⁴ _____

---

b Complete the application form with information about you.

HARLOW SPORTS CLUB

To join HSC, please complete this form.

Personal details

Title: _____

Surname: _____

First name: _____

Nationality: _____

Date of birth: _____
(dd/mm/yyyy)

Contact details

Address: _____

Email address: _____

Phone (mobile):   _____

Phone (home):   _____

Signature: _____

Date: *(dd/mm/yyyy)*   _____

Language live
Answering questions

13a Complete the questions with the words in the box.

'*s*   your   what   are   that   got   spell

1 What ___'s___ your name?
2 Can you say _____ again, please?
3 How do you _____ that?
4 _____'s your address?
5 What's _____ postcode?
6 Have you _____ a contact phone number?
7 How old _____ you?

b Match questions 1–7 in exercise a with answers a–g.

a I'm 22.   ☐ 7
b BS9 1EB.   ☐
c 07937 883220.   ☐
d It's Luis Cordoba.   ☐
e L-U-I-S   C-O-R-D-O-B-A.   ☐
f Yes, of course. Luis Cordoba.   ☐
g 23 Bonsal Avenue, Bristol.   ☐

c 🎧 **2.8** Listen and check.

d 🎧 **2.9** Listen to the questions. Say the answers for you.

14 Write a similar conversation. Use the phrases in exercise 13 and your own ideas.

_____
_____
_____
_____
_____
_____
_____
_____
_____

Vocabulary
Common verbs

1 Match verbs 1–6 with the words and phrases in the box. Write three words/phrases for each verb.

~~very hard~~   ~~at home~~   ~~in a big city~~
with my parents   to work by bus   to bed late
early on weekdays   breakfast at home   out a lot
in a flat   lunch in a café   a bath in the evening
late at the weekend   economics   at university
in an office   for a small company   at 6:30 a.m.

1 live   _in a big city_
2 study   _very hard_
3 work   _at home_
4 have   _____
5 go   _____
6 get up   _____

2 Complete the questions with one word.

1 I ___have___ a shower in the evening.
2 My sister gets _____ early at the weekend.
3 Ben and James go _____ school by bus.
4 Lisa and her friends _____ out a lot in the evenings.
5 We work _____ a big company.
6 I live _____ my parents.
7 They don't study _____ the evening.
8 I go _____ bed late at the weekend.
9 I don't _____ English at university.
10 We don't _____ breakfast at home.

Grammar focus 1
Present simple: positive and negative (*I, you, we, they*)

3a Put the words in the correct order to make sentences.

1 early / I get / up
   I get up early.
2 You / nearby / live
   _____
3 have / a / They / new / number / phone
   _____
4 very / hard / We / work
   _____
5 a / memory / I / stick / have
   _____
6 live / We / in / of / flats / block/ a
   _____
7 university / They / at / study / French
   _____
8 bus / We / school / go / to / by
   _____
9 lunch / a / in / café / They / have
   _____
10 You / the / go / in / out / evening
   _____

b 🎧 **3.1 Listen and check.**

4a Match the sentence halves.

1 Most people don't work   `b`
2 Maoris don't come from   ☐
3 People in Brazil don't speak   ☐
4 Babies don't go   ☐
5 Most children don't study   ☐
6 Vegetarians don't eat   ☐

a economics.
b at the weekend.
c Australia.
d meat.
e to school.
f Spanish.

b 🎧 **3.2 Listen and check. Practise saying the sentences.**

5a Complete the sentences with the negative form of the verb in the second sentence.

1 I _____*don't work*_____ in an office. I work at home.
2 Bob and Jackie _____ in a city. They live in a small town.
3 We _____ economics. We study computer science.
4 My friends and I _____ to university by car. We go by bus.
5 I _____ on weekdays. I go out at the weekend.
6 You _____ a small flat! You have a beautiful big flat!
7 I _____ a shower in the morning. I have a bath in the evening.
8 My cousins _____ in an office. They work in a shopping centre.

b 🎧 3.3 Listen and check.

6a Look at the tables and complete the sentences about Erik and Anna from Sweden and Julia and Ken from Singapore.

Erik and Anna

Home	a five-bedroom house in a small town in Sweden
Languages	Swedish, English, German
Jobs	lawyers
Hobbies	the cinema
Drinks	mineral water and coffee
Food	Swedish and Italian food

1 Erik and Anna *don't live* in a big city.
2 They _____ in a big house.
3 They _____ English.
4 They _____ Chinese.
5 They _____ in a school.
6 They _____ to the cinema a lot.

Julia and Ken

Home	a small flat in the centre of Singapore city
Languages	English, Chinese, Malay
Jobs	teachers
Hobbies	eating in restaurants
Drinks	tea
Food	Chinese food

7 Julia and Ken _____*live*_____ in a big city.
8 They _____ in a big house.
9 They _____ Chinese and English.
10 They _____ in an office.
11 They _____ in a school.
12 They _____ to the cinema a lot.

b Write more sentences about Erik and Anna and Julia and Ken.

Erik and Anna
1 They _____ .
2 They _____ .
3 They _____ .

Julia and Ken
4 They _____ .
5 They _____ .
6 They _____ .

Grammar focus 2
Present simple: questions and short answers (*I, you, we, they*)

7a **Look at the tables in exercise 6 again and write short answers to the questions.**

1 **A:** Do Erik and Anna live in a small town?
   B: *Yes, they do.*
2 **A:** Do they work in an office?
   B: _____
3 **A:** Do they speak Chinese?
   B: _____
4 **A:** Do they drink tea?
   B: _____
5 **A:** Do Julia and Ken live in a big city?
   B: _____
6 **A:** Do they go to the cinema a lot?
   B: _____
7 **A:** Do they eat Italian food?
   B: _____
8 **A:** Do they drink tea?
   B: _____

b **Answer the questions about you.**

1 **A:** Do you live in a small town?
   B: *No, I don't.*
2 **A:** Do you work in an office?
   B: _____
3 **A:** Do you speak Chinese?
   B: _____
4 **A:** Do you drink tea?
   B: _____
5 **A:** Do you live in a big city?
   B: _____
6 **A:** Do you go to the cinema a lot?
   B: _____
7 **A:** Do you eat Italian food?
   B: _____
8 **A:** Do you drink tea?
   B: _____

8a **Put the words in the correct order to make questions.**

1 Do / in a big city / you / live ?
   Do you live in a big city?
2 food / you / and / your friends / like / Chinese / Do ?
   _____
3 Do / economics / you / study ?
   _____
4 hard / I / work / Do ?
   _____
5 in a nice town / Do / live / we ?
   _____
6 email / got / Have / you / address / an ?
   _____
7 up / you / early / in the morning / Do / get ?
   _____
8 Do / English / your / speak / cousins ?
   _____

b **Match questions 1–10 in exercise a with answers a–j.**

a No, I don't. I'm not a student.   3
b Yes, I do. There are nine million people in Bangkok.   ☐
c Yes, we do. I think it's beautiful.   ☐
d No, I don't. I work in the evening and I get up late.   ☐
e Yes, I have. It's jhf@biggmail.com.   ☐
f Yes, you do. You're a very good student!   ☐
g Yes, we do. We go to Chinese restaurants every weekend.   ☐
h Yes, they do. They speak English and Italian.   ☐

c 🎧 **3.4 Listen and check.**

Pronunciation
Sentence stress in questions

9 🎧 **3.5 Listen and look at the stress. Which one is correct?**

1 a Do you study at university?   ✈
  b Do you study at university?   ___
2 a Do you have a watch?   ___
  b Do you have a watch?   ___
3 a Do you get up early?   ___
  b Do you get up early?   ___
4 a Do we have a lesson today?   ___
  b Do we have a lesson today?   ___
5 a Do you go by car?   ___
  b Do you go by car?   ___
6 a Do you have a big family?   ___
  b Do you have a big family?   ___
7 a Do they live with you?   ___
  b Do they live with you?   ___
8 a Do they go to restaurants?   ___
  b Do they go to restaurants?   ___

Vocabulary
Telling the time

10 Look at the pictures and write the times.

1 _It's ten past eight._   **2** _____

3 _____   **4** _____

5 _____   **6** _____

7 _____   **8** _____

9 _____

11a Match the times 1–8 with a–h.

1 6:20   d
2 6:35
3 8:10
4 9:00
5 5:15
6 6:15
7 8:30
8 10:45

a ten past eight
b quarter past six
c half past eight
d twenty past six
e twenty-five to seven
f quarter to eleven
g nine o'clock
h quarter past five

b Write sentences about Hiroki's day. Use the times in exercise a.

1 6:20 : get up
Hiroki gets up at twenty past six.

2 6:35: breakfast

_____

3 8:10: go to work

_____

4 9:00: start work

_____

5 5:15: finish work

_____

6 6:15: leave swimming pool and go home

_____

7 8:30: dinner

_____

8 10:45: bed

_____

12 Complete the sentences with *in*, *at* or *to*.

1 It's seven o'clock ___*in*___ the morning.
2 Do you have a big lunch _____ Sunday?
3 I get up _____ six o'clock.
4 We work from eight to eleven _____ the morning.
5 Shops don't stay open _____ night.
6 I finish work at eight o'clock _____ the evening.
7 Do you go out a lot _____ the weekend?
8 The children don't sleep _____ the afternoon.

Places in a town

13 Complete the sentences with the words in the box.

....
beach   block of flats
swimming pool   restaurant
supermarket   cinema
shopping centre   park
....

1 In summer I go to the _____*beach*_____ and swim in the sea. But in the winter it's cold, so I go to the _____ in my town.
2 My home is in a _____ . I live on the fourth floor.
3 My street has got a lovely Italian _____ . The pizzas are great.
4 I buy all my fruit, vegetables, meat and fish in the _____ near my flat.
5 Zara loves films. She goes to the _____ every week.
6 Hamton City has got a new _____ . It's got fifty shops and a big car park.
7 My town has got a big _____ in the centre. The trees are beautiful and I play football there.

Listen and read

14a 🎧 3.6 **Read and listen to the text about young people in South Korea.**

Studying in South Korea

What time do you have breakfast?

Where do you have lunch?

Do you go out with your friends for a coffee after school or after work?

Do you work in the evenings or do you have dinner with family or friends?

Life is very different for many young people in South Korea. It's very important for people to go to a good university and find a good job, so study is very, very important! Young people get up at about six o'clock, have breakfast with their family and then go to school. Schools in South Korea start at seven o'clock.

After five hours of lessons in the morning, it's time for lunch. Most people have lunch at school. Then there are more lessons until four o'clock, but that's not the end! Many young Koreans go to the library and study after school or go to extra classes until ten o'clock.

At that time, they go home in a special minibus. Most students don't go to bed before one or two o'clock and then, the next day, after just four or five hours of sleep, it's time to get up again.

b **Read the text again and answer the questions.**

1 What time do most young people in South Korea get up?
   They get up at six o'clock.
2 What time do schools in South Korea start?
   _____
3 Where do most young people have lunch?
   _____
4 What time do schools in South Korea finish?
   _____
5 Where do many young people go in the evening?
   _____
6 What time do the libraries close?
   _____
7 How do students go home?
   _____
8 What time do they go to bed?
   _____

Grammar focus 1

Present simple: positive and negative (*he/she/it*)

1 Add letters to complete the *he/she/it* form of the verbs.

1 My mother read<u>s</u> *Hi!* magazine.
2 James watch _ _ TV in the morning.
3 Winnie come _ from South Korea.
4 Richard live _ in the United States.
5 She go _ _ to bed at eleven o'clock.
6 He enjoy _ watching football on TV.
7 My brother say _ he's fine.
8 She fl _ _ _ _ to London every summer – she never goes by train.
9 Tom always play _ football on Saturday.

2a Look at the table and complete the sentences about Akiko with the Present simple form of the verb in brackets.

	Akiko Murata	David Jones	Lauren Andersen	Tomasz Nowak
Nationality	Japanese	British	Australian	Polish
Job	fashion designer	English teacher	bank employee	music teacher
Address	Golden Gate Avenue, San Francisco	The English School, Seoul, South Korea	Carrer Bonavista, Barcelona, Spain	Rue d'Alleray, Paris, France
Languages	Japanese, English	English, Italian, Korean	Spanish, Catalan, English	Polish, French, Russian
Hobbies	cooking, dancing	watching football, playing the guitar	reading, going to the gym	playing computer games, swimming, going for walks

1 She _comes from_ (come from) from Japan.
2 She _____ (work) as a fashion designer.
3 She _____ (live) in San Francisco.
4 She _____ (speak) Japanese and English.
5 She _____ (like) cooking and dancing.

b 🎧 **4.1 Listen and check. Practise saying the sentences.**

3 Look at the table in exercise 2a. Write sentences about David, Lauren and Tomasz using the Present simple.

1 David _teaches English_____ . (teach)
2 He _____ .
(come from)
3 _____
(live)
4 _____
(speak)
5 _____
(play)
6 Lauren _lives in Spain_____ . (live)
7 She _____ .
(come from)
8 _____
(speak)
9 _____
(work)
10 _____
(go to the gym)
11 Tomasz _speaks Polish, French and Russian_ . (speak)
12 He _____ .
(come from)
13 _____
(live)
14 _____
(teach)
15 _____
(play)

4a Make the sentences negative.

1 Maria likes studying grammar.
_Maria doesn't like studying grammar.____
2 It rains in summer.
_____
3 My brother likes getting up at seven o'clock.
_____
4 The restaurant closes on Sunday evening.
_____
5 Martin comes to class every week.
_____
6 Tony buys all his food at the supermarket.
_____
7 Carla drives to work.
_____
8 My cousin visits me every month.
_____

b 🎧 **4.2 Listen and check. Practise saying the sentences.**

5 Complete the text with the Present simple form of the verbs in brackets.

Malcolm Tracey ¹*doesn't go* (not go) to work; he only ² _____ (leave) his hometown to go on holiday in the Caribbean. But Malcolm is a millionaire. He ³ _____ (write) books about money and how to make a lot of it. His new book is called *Easy Money: How to make money without getting out of bed*. Malcolm ⁴ _____ (live) in a large house near London. He ⁵ _____ (get up) at about eight o'clock in the morning and ⁶ _____ (have) breakfast with his family. After breakfast, he ⁷ _____ (drive) his children to school and ⁸ _____ (read) the newspaper in the garden until lunchtime. After lunch, he ⁹ _____ (buy) and ¹⁰ _____ (sell) on the internet. He ¹¹ _____ (finish) work at four o'clock when his children come home. 'I've got a simple system for making money,' Malcolm ¹² _____ (say). 'It ¹³ _____ (not work) for everybody, but it ¹⁴ _____ (work) for me!'

6 Read about Irene and Agnes. Write sentences about the things they like and dislike.

Irene and Agnes are both au pairs. They live with a family, do housework (clean the house) and help with the children. In the afternoon, they take an English course. In the evenings, they often babysit.

....

☹ ☹ = It's horrible! I hate it!

☹ = I don't like it.

☺ = I like it.

☺ ☺ = It's fantastic! I love it!

....

	Irene	Agnes
taking the children to school	☹	☺
housework	☹ ☹	☺ ☺
talking to the family	☺ ☺	☹
the English course	☹	☹ ☹
babysitting	☹	☺

1 (taking the children to school)
   Irene doesn't like taking the children to school.
   Agnes likes taking the children to school.
2 (housework)
   Irene _____
   Agnes _____
3 (talking to the family)
   Irene _____
   Agnes _____
4 (the English course)
   Irene _____
   Agnes _____
5 (babysitting)
   Irene _____
   Agnes _____

Vocabulary
Activities

7 Add letters to complete the activities in the text.

> At the weekend, I really like being outside.
> I love ¹g <u>o i n</u> g for ²w _ _ _ _ s.
> I love ³spe _ _ _ _ _ time with friends.
> My friends and I have got bikes and we like
> ⁴c _ _ _ _ _ _ g. We also go to nightclubs –
> I love ⁵dan _ _ _ _ _ . I don't like
> ⁶r _ _ _ _ _ _ g books, but magazines are OK!
> And I've got a new computer – I don't like
> ⁷pla _ _ _ _ _ computer ⁸g _ _ _ _ s, but I love
> spending ⁹t _ _ _ on the internet. And I love
> ¹⁰wat _ _ _ _ _ _ sport on TV. Football is my
> number one sport!

8 Complete the sentences with the verbs in the box.

....
~~plays~~   swimming   spending   cooking
watch   cycle   goes   reading
....

1 My brother Hector _____*plays*_____ a lot of computer games.

2 'Do you like _____ the newspaper?' 'No, I don't. I watch the news on TV.'

3 'Do you like _____ in the sea?' 'No, it's too cold.'

4 My mother and father always _____ sport on TV at the weekend.

5 'Do you enjoy _____ time on the internet?' 'Yes, I love it.'

6 Derek _____ for walks in the park every day.

7 I've got a new bike and I _____ to university every day.

8 My sister hates _____ , but she loves eating!

Vocabulary
Phrases for time and frequency

9 Complete the sentences with *in*, *on* or *at*.

1 I often go for a run ____*in*____ the morning.

2 I'm sometimes bored _____ the afternoon.

3 I usually work _____ weekdays.

4 But I sometimes work _____ weekends, too.

5 I'm always tired when I get home from work _____ the evening.

6 I never drink coffee _____ night.

7 I usually go to the supermarket _____ Saturdays.

10 Choose the correct answers.

1 In the morning, the sun (always)/ *never* / *sometimes* comes up in the east.

2 Sharks *never* / *sometimes* / *often* kill people.

3 Children *never* / *don't often* / *usually* like sweets.

4 In the game of chess, black *always* / *never* / *usually* starts.

5 People with brown hair *don't often* / *never* / *often* have brown eyes.

6 Monday *always* / *often* / *usually* comes before Tuesday.

7 A week *always* / *never* / *usually* has eight days.

8 Spiders *always* / *often* / *sometimes* have eight legs.

11 Write the word in brackets in the correct place in the sentences.

sometimes
1 I ∧ have dinner at my friend's house. (sometimes)

2 Caroline eats fish. (never)

3 I often eat in a restaurant. (don't)

4 I get up late on a Sunday morning. (usually)

5 It's very hot in August in my city. (always)

6 The Brown family usually to Italy on holiday. (go)

7 The weather always cold in January. (is)

8 The bus is late. (often)

12 Choose the correct answers.

1 (She's always) / Always she's here on Mondays.
2 My friends and I **go often out** / **often go out** at the weekends.
3 The food in this restaurant **is always good** / **good always is**.
4 We **are never** / **never are** late for work.
5 I work in the hospital in the evenings, so I **never** / **usually** come home late from work.
6 My brother is a vegetarian, so he **often** / **never** eats meat.
7 I love films, so I **sometimes** / **never** go to the cinema.
8 The sun **often** / **always** sets in the west.

Listen and read

13 🎧 4.3 Read and listen to the text about English people's homes abroad.

An Englishman's home ...

'An Englishman's home,' they say, 'is his castle.' Perhaps that's true, but nowadays the home often isn't in England – it's abroad!

More than half a million British people have a second home in another country. Many buy old houses in the south of France or in Tuscany, in the north of Italy. The Eurostar train, which goes from London to Paris in two and a half hours, makes it easy to go from one home to the other quickly.

The Noteman family, who live in London, have got a small house in Gascony. They sometimes go there for weekends and they always spend the summer in France with their four children. Jerry Noteman says, 'We really like living in France: the weather is usually good, we like the food and the people are very friendly. We don't usually speak French when we go out – most of our neighbours in the village are English, too!'

14 Read the text again and answer the questions.

1 How many British people have a home abroad?
   More than half a million.
2 Where do they often buy houses?
   _____
3 Where does the Eurostar train go?
   _____
4 Where do the Noteman family live in England?
   _____
5 Where do they live in France?
   _____
6 Where do they spend the summer?
   _____
7 How many children do they have?
   _____
8 What do they like about living in France?
   _____
9 Where do most of their neighbours come from?
   _____

Grammar focus 2
Present simple: questions and short answers (*he/she/it*)

15a Put the words in the correct order to make questions.

1 Does / sister / cycle / your ?
   Does your sister cycle?
2 sports / Does / play / she ?
   _____
3 Does / cooking / your / boyfriend / like ?
   _____
4 you / often / Does / he / cook / for ?
   _____
5 got / car / a / big / your / father / Has ?
   _____
6 it / go / Does / fast ?
   _____

b Match questions 1–6 in exercise a with answers a–f.

a Yes, he has. It's very big.   [5]
b No, it doesn't. It's old and slow.   ☐
c Yes, he does. He's a very good cook. ☐
d No, he doesn't. I usually cook for him! ☐
e No, she doesn't. She doesn't have a bike. ☐
f Yes, she does. She plays tennis and basketball. ☐

c 🎧 4.4 Listen and check.

16a Complete the questions about Olaf.

1 **A:** *Where* does he live?
B: He lives in Oslo.
2 **A:** What _____ he do?
B: He's an engineer.
3 **A:** Where does _____ work?
B: He works in the city centre.
4 **A:** How does he _____ to work?
B: He goes to work by bike.
5 **A:** _____ does Olaf's wife do?
B: She's a doctor.
6 **A:** How _____ he spend his weekends?
B: He spends his weekends with his family.

b 🎧 **4.5** Listen and check.

17 Find and correct the mistakes in the questions. Three questions are correct.

1 Does Fred likes his job? ☐
Does Fred like his job?
2 How often does she go swimming? ☑
_____
3 What does your wife do? ☐
_____
4 Where do your brother live? ☐
_____
5 Does she gets up late at the weekend? ☐
_____
6 Does she like reading in her free time? ☐
_____

Pronunciation
Strong and weak forms of *does*

18a 🎧 **4.6** Listen to the pronunciation of *does* in the questions and short answers. Practise saying them.

1 Does she get up early at the weekend?
a /dʌz/   **ⓑ** /dəz/
2 Yes, she does. But she hasn't got much free time.
a /dʌz/   **b** /dəz/
3 Where does Julie work?
a /dʌz/   **b** /dəz/
4 How often does she go to the cinema?
a /dʌz/   **b** /dəz/
5 Does she like reading in her free time?
a /dʌz/   **b** /dəz/
6 Yes, she does. But she doesn't have much free time.
a /dʌz/   **b** /dəz/

b Listen again. How is *does* pronounced: /dʌz/ or /dəz/? Choose the correct answer, a or b.

Language live
Meeting people

19a Complete the conversations with the phrases in the box.

....
~~This is~~   these are for you   Nice to meet you
I'm fine   Yes, please   Would you like
They're lovely
....

1 **A:** Hi, Bea. _____ *This is* _____
Clara. She's my friend from university.
B: Hello, Clara. I'm Bea.
_____ .
C: Nice to meet you, too.
2 **A:** Happy birthday! I know you like flowers, so
_____ .
B: Oh, what nice flowers! Thank you so much!
_____ !
3 **A:** _____ something to drink?
B: _____ . An orange juice, please.
A: And a drink for you, Henri?
C: No, thanks, _____ .

b 🎧 **4.7** Listen and check.

Writing
Introducing a friend

20a Read the email from your friend Francis. Where is his new job?

Hello,

How are you?

I have some news! I've got a new job as a lawyer in Chicago! I start next month. I love spending time with my friends and dancing and going to museums, but I don't know anyone in Chicago. I want to make friends in the city. Do you know anyone there?

Love,
Francis

b Your friend Sam lives in Chicago. Francis wants to make friends in Chicago. Write an email to Sam and introduce Francis.

Tell Sam:
• what Francis does.
• what Francis likes doing.

Vocabulary
Transport

1 Add letters to complete the types of transport.

1 b <u>u</u> s

2 m _ t _ r b _ k _

3 s c _ _ t _ r

4 b _ c _ cl _

5 pl _ n _

6 t r _ m

7 t r _ _ n

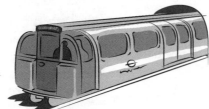

8 _ n d _ r g r _ _ n d t r _ _ n

9 t _ x _

Listen and read

2 🎧 **5.1** Read and listen to the text about transport statistics.

Transport statistics

6	is the number of hours it takes to travel from London to New York by plane.
44	is the number of platforms at New York's Grand Central Terminal station. About 700,000 people use the station every day.
300	kilometres an hour is the speed of the Spanish AVE train, which goes from the capital city Madrid to Seville, in the south of Spain, a distance of 470 kilometres. The journey takes about two and a half hours.
524	is the number of passengers who can travel in a Boeing 747-400 plane. It can fly for more than 13,000 kilometres without stopping. That's from London to Tokyo and back again.
9,288	kilometres is the distance of the Trans-Siberian railway, which goes from Moscow to the town of Vladivostok in eastern Russia. The journey takes about seven days.
60,000	is the number of taxis in Mexico City.
6,300,000	is the total kilometres of roads in the United States.
70,000,000	is the number of people who travel through London Heathrow Airport every year.

3 Read the text again and answer the questions.

1 How long does it take to travel from Madrid to Seville by the AVE train?
Two and a half hours.

2 Where does the Trans-Siberian railway begin?
_____

3 How many people can travel on a Boeing 747-400?
_____

4 Which country has 6,300,000 kilometres of road?
_____

5 How many people pass through Heathrow Airport every year?
_____

6 Which city has 60,000 taxis?
_____

7 Which railway station has forty-four platforms?
_____

8 How long does it take to fly from London to New York?
_____

Vocabulary
Travelling

4 Match words and phrases 1–7 with their meanings a–g.

1 destination | d |
2 delayed | |
3 book a ticket online | |
4 board the plane | |
5 your luggage | |
6 Departures | |
7 boarding pass | |

a late
b buy your journey on the internet
c bags with you on your journey
d the place that you are going to
e get onto the plane before your flight
f the place in the airport where you wait for your flight
g plane ticket with your seat number; you get it when you check in

5a Complete the sentences with the words in the box.

> ~~boarding pass~~   gate   go through   flight   luggage   board
> Departures   destination

1 Thank you, sir. Here's your _boarding pass_ . You have seat 17C.
2 Show your passport again when you _____ security.
3 Please wait in _____ . Your flight is in one hour.
4 Look at the screen. There's our flight: KLM267 to Amsterdam, from _____ 14. Let's go!
5 The plane is now ready. People with small children, please _____ the plane now.
6 Good morning, everyone, this is your pilot. Welcome on our _____ to Amsterdam.
7 Hello again, everyone. This is your pilot. We are now at our _____ . Welcome to Amsterdam!
8 Excuse me, I can't find my _____ – one suitcase and a blue bag.

b 🎧 5.2 Listen and check.

Grammar focus 1
can/can't: possibility and ability

6 Look at the motorway signs and complete the sentences with *can* or *can't*.

1 You _can't_ stop on the motorway.
2 You _____ drive at 100 kilometres an hour.
3 You _____ drive at 180 kilometres an hour.
4 You _____ ride a bicycle on the motorway.
5 You _____ walk on the motorway.
6 You _____ find something to eat and drink at the service station.
7 You _____ buy petrol at the service station.
8 You _____ turn round.
9 Learner drivers _____ use the motorway.

7a Look at the signs and write short answers to the questions.

NO PARKING
MONDAY - SATURDAY 9.30 - 5.30

1 A: It's 8:30 in the morning. Can I park here?
   B: *Yes, you can.*

2 A: Can I park here on a Sunday?
   B: _____

NO SMOKING

3 A: Can I smoke here?
   B: _____

SORRY No children under 18

4 A: Tom and Barbara are sixteen years old. Can they go in?
   B: _____

5 A: I'm nineteen years old. Can I go in?
   B: _____

WALK

6 A: Can I cross the road now?
   B: _____

NO DOGS

7 A: I've got a dog. Can it come in?
   B: _____

PHONECARDS For Sale HERE

8 A: Excuse me, can we buy a phonecard here?
   B: _____

b 🎧 5.3 Listen and check. Practise saying the questions and answers.

8a Look at the table and complete the sentences about Caroline and Fabrizio.

	speak French	play chess	drive a car	play a musical instrument
Caroline	✓	✗	✗	✓
Fabrizio	✓	✓	✗	✗
Kristina	✗	✗	✓	✓
Max	✗	✓	✓	✗

1 Caroline __can__ speak French.
2 She _can't_ play chess.
3 She _____ drive a car.
4 She _____ play a musical instrument.
5 Fabrizio _____ .
6 He _____ .
7 He _____ .
8 He _____ .

b 🎧 5.4 Listen and check. Practise saying the sentences.

9a Look at the table in exercise 8a again and write questions and short answers about Kristina and Max.

1 A: *Can Kristina speak French?*
   B: *No, she can't.*

2 A: _____
   B: _____

3 A: _____
   B: _____

4 A: _____
   B: _____

5 A: _____
   B: _____

6 A: _____
   B: _____

7 A: _____
   B: _____

8 A: _____
   B: _____

b 🎧 5.5 Listen and check. Practise saying the questions and answers.

Pronunciation
can/can't

10 🎧 **5.6** Listen to the pronunciation of *can* and *can't* in the sentences. Write the sentence numbers in the table.

/kən/	/kæn/	/kɑːnt/
1	2	3

1 Can you speak Japanese?
2 Yes, I can.
3 I can't read Chinese.
4 We can get the bus.
5 They can play tennis.
6 You can't play golf.
7 Can she read music?
8 Yes, she can.
9 Can you play the piano?
10 No, I can't.
11 I can't swim.
12 My brother can drive a car.
13 Can you eat and drink here?
14 No, you can't.

Grammar focus 2
Articles: *a/an*, *the* and no article

11 Complete the sentences with *a* or *the*.

1 Can you ride ____*a*____ bicycle?
2 Does it take a long time to get to _____ city centre?
3 I always drive to work, but _____ lot of people come by underground.
4 She's _____ teacher in school in New York.
5 The traffic is very bad in _____ evening.
6 My uncle is _____ train driver.
7 'Have you got _____ car?' 'No, I haven't.'
8 We live in _____ small town in _____ United States.

12 Cross out the extra *the* in each sentence.

1 Parking is very difficult in the city centre, so I always go there by ~~the~~ bus.
2 Eight o'clock is a good time to phone Thomas: he's always at the home in the evening.
3 It's so cold in the city centre today that a lot of people can't go to the work.
4 The train times are different on the Sundays.
5 What do you think of the public transport in the London?
6 You can use a railcard in most of the countries in the Europe.
7 I live in the Dubai in the United Arab Emirates.
8 Our plane arrives in Los Angeles at the two o'clock in the afternoon.

13a Complete the quiz questions with *a/an*, *the* or – (no article).

QUIZ

1 What is __*the*__ capital of Colombia?
2 In _____ India, do people drive on _____ left or on _____ right?
3 Which languages do they speak in _____ Canada?
4 How many grams are there in _____ kilogram?
5 Where is _____ Haneda Airport?
6 Who is _____ Daniel Craig?
7 How far is it from _____ Earth to _____ Moon?
8 How long does it take to boil _____ egg?
9 What are the four countries in _____ UK?
10 What's the name of _____ big river in Budapest?

b Can you answer the questions in exercise a?

c 🎧 **5.7** Listen and check. You will hear the questions and the answers.

14a Write *a* or *the* in the correct place in the sentences.

        a
1 Zara is ∧ doctor in a hospital in the centre of Baghdad.
2 My cousin Alfred lives in United States.
3 I've got two brothers and sister.
4 What do you like doing at weekend?
5 My family and I usually watch TV in evening.
6 I've got scooter, but I go to my office in the morning by bus.
7 You can take taxi or go by bus to the airport.
8 I love spending my time on internet.
9 Jake is a professional musician and he lives in flat in Milan.
10 I spend four hours a week on London Underground. I hate it!

b 🎧 **5.8** Listen and check.

06 FOOD AND DRINK

Vocabulary
Food: countable and uncountable nouns

1a Find 11 more words for food and drink in the word square.

W	A	G	R	D	R	C	L	S	B	R	E
S	A	N	D	W	I	C	H	M	O	T	G
R	P	O	G	R	C	H	I	C	K	E	N
B	P	B	B	N	W	E	A	F	T	W	E
R	L	T	O	H	N	E	T	R	G	A	E
E	E	G	G	B	I	S	C	U	I	T	P
A	F	W	I	A	C	E	E	I	H	E	U
D	H	A	L	N	E	B	A	T	G	R	Z
U	T	O	M	A	T	O	H	B	A	N	H
X	P	K	L	N	E	U	T	I	G	N	U
O	S	G	R	A	P	E	F	C	H	E	P
V	P	T	I	D	K	E	M	P	M	A	L

b Write the words from the word square in exercise a in the correct group.

Drinks: _____

Types of fruit: _____

Other things you can eat: _sandwich_ _____

_____

2a Circle the uncountable nouns in the box.

bread   egg   sandwich   biscuit   olive oil
chicken   apple   fruit   grape   cheese
orange juice   salad   banana   water   tomato

b Complete the crossword. Use ten words from exercise a. Add -s/-es to the countable nouns.

1 These are red. People think they're vegetables, but they are not!
2 People in Mediterranean countries cook with this healthy oil. (2 words)
3 This is the world's number one drink.
4 These can be red or light green.
5 These have two pieces of bread and something in the middle.
6 This is healthy and green. You don't cook it.
7 These come from birds and people eat them.
8 This is a healthy kind of food, for example apples, grapes and bananas.
9 People make this from milk.
10 These are yellow and about 15 cm long.

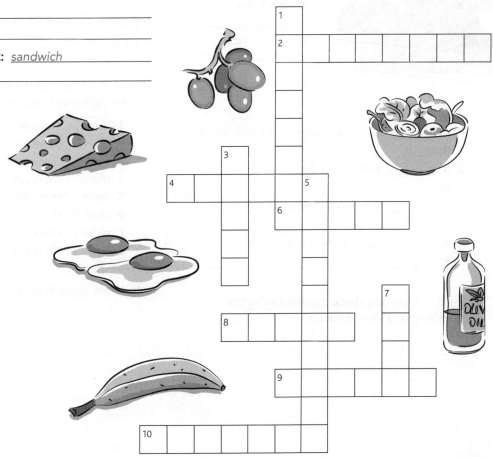

29

Grammar focus 1

there is and *there are*; *some* and *any*

3 Complete the sentences with the correct form of *there is* or *there are*.

1 *Is there* _____ any milk in the fridge?
2 How many students _____ in your class?
3 _____ a very good beach near our hotel.
4 _____ any cheap restaurants near here?
5 _____ a university in Brighton?
6 I'm sorry, but _____ any shops open at this time.
7 _____ 50 states in the USA.
8 _____ any milk, sorry. How about lemon in your tea?

4a Read about the campsite. Complete the questions and write short answers.

1 **A:** ___*Is*___ there a swimming pool?
  B: ___*Yes, there is.*___

Las Molinas

÷ **swimming pool**

÷ **tennis courts**

÷ **restaurant, drinks bar**

÷ **children's playground**

÷ **10 km from the historic town of Los Pozos**

2 **A:** _____ there any places to eat and drink?
  B: _____
3 **A:** _____ there a beach?
  B: _____
4 **A:** _____ there a children's playground?
  B: _____
5 **A:** _____ there any supermarkets?
  B: _____

b 🎧 **6.1 Listen and check. Practise saying the questions and short answers.**

5a Choose the correct answers.

1 **A:** Mum, I'm hungry. Are there [1]**some /(any)** biscuits?
  B: No, there [2]**isn't / aren't**. Have [3]**some / any** fruit.
2 **A:** Good morning. [4]**Is / Are** there any Swiss cheese?
  B: No, there [5]**isn't / aren't** any Swiss cheese. But we've got [6]**some / any** English cheese.
  A: Oh, good. Can I have [7]**some / any** English cheese, please? About 200 grams, please.
3 **A:** That pizza looks lovely. [8]**Is / Are** there any meat on it?
  B: No, there [9]**isn't / aren't**.
  A: Oh, good. I don't eat meat, you see. Can I have [10]**some / any** pizza, please?

b 🎧 **6.2 Listen and check.**

6 Complete the sentences with *some* or *any*.

1 Have you got __*any*__ orange juice?
2 There are _____ letters here for you.
3 There's _____ salt, but there isn't _____ pepper.
4 We haven't got _____ eggs.
5 Would you like _____ milk in your coffee?
6 Are there _____ knives on the table?
7 We haven't got _____ more bread. Would you like _____ biscuits with your cheese?
8 I'm sorry, we haven't got _____ hot food, but we've got _____ sandwiches if you're hungry.

Pronunciation

there is and *there are*

7a 🎧 **6.3 Listen to the sentences. Do you hear *there's* or *there are*? Choose the correct answers.**

1 (**there's**)/ **there are**
2 **there's / there are**
3 **there's / there are**
4 **there's / there are**
5 **there's / there are**
6 **there's / there are**
7 **there's / there are**
8 **there's / there are**

b Listen again. Practise saying the sentences.

Listen and read

8a 🎧 **6.4 Listen and read the article about Annaprashan.**

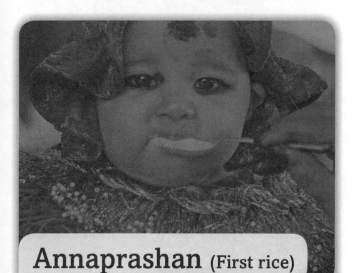

Annaprashan (First rice)

Who celebrates Annaprashan?
Annaprashan is a special day for Hindu families with a young baby. Annaprashan happens in many different countries all over the world, including India, Nepal, Sri Lanka, Indonesia and Mauritius.

What is Annaprashan?
In English, the Annaprashan ceremony is called 'First rice'. The family meets and it is the first time the baby has food. The baby eats rice with milk and sugar.

What do babies eat?
When babies are very young, they can only drink their mother's milk. But when they are about six months old, they need different kinds of food. They need vitamins and protein. There are a lot of vitamins and protein in fish. But it isn't a good baby food because fish bones are dangerous. When babies are six months old, they don't have teeth, so they need very soft food. Rice is soft and healthy and babies usually like rice.

What happens at an Annaprashan ceremony?
The baby sits with his or her mother. First, a man from the baby's family (an uncle or grandfather) gives the baby some food on a spoon. Then the rest of the family give the baby more food. And then they play a game: the baby chooses a toy and plays with it, and the adults decide the baby's future job!

b Read the text again. Are the statements true (T) or false (F)?

1 Annaprashan is a family celebration. [T]
2 Annaprashan ceremonies happen in lots of different countries. ☐
3 Babies eat at Annaprashan ceremonies. ☐
4 Fish is a good baby food. ☐
5 Babies have teeth when they are six months old. ☐
6 The English name for 'Annaprashan' is 'baby food'. ☐
7 At an Annaprashan ceremony, the baby gets food from his or her family. ☐

Vocabulary
Food pairs

9a Tick (✓) the correct food pairs. Correct the incorrect ones.

1 chips and fish   _fish and chips_
2 fruit and vegetables   ___✓___
3 herbs and spices   _____
4 sour and sweet   _____
5 knife and fork   _____
6 tea and coffee   _____
7 drink and food   _____
8 salt and pepper   _____
9 butter and bread   _____

b 🎧 **6.5 Listen and check.**

10a Complete the sentences with food pairs from exercise 9a.

1 **A:** My son is three. He eats with a plastic _knife and fork_ .
   B: Really? My daughter just eats with her hands!
2 **A:** I want a sandwich. We've got some cheese, but is there any _____ ?
   B: No, there isn't. Have an apple!
3 **A:** Hi, it's me. I'm in the supermarket. Do we need any _____ ?
   B: Yes, we do. Grapes and carrots, please.
4 **A:** I love cooking with _____ . Garlic, pepper and turmeric are my favourites.
   B: Really? Well, you can cook dinner tonight, then!
5 **A:** When you go to the mountains, take lots of _____ with you. There aren't any shops in the mountains.
   B: Yes, Mum!
6 **A:** What would you like to drink with your breakfast, sir? We've got fruit juice and _____ , of course.
   B: A black coffee, please.

b 🎧 **6.6 Listen and check.**

Grammar focus 2

how much and *how many*

11a Put the words in the correct order to make questions.

1　How / sugar / is / much / there ?
　　How much sugar is there?

2　do / you / How / much / meat / eat ?
　　_____
　　_____

3　potatoes and carrots / How / there / many / are ?
　　_____
　　_____

4　in / How / is / much / fat / there / cheese ?
　　_____
　　_____

5　How / can / eat / much / we / salt ?
　　_____
　　_____

6　How / eggs / do / I / many / need ?
　　_____
　　_____

7　would / you / How / like / much / coffee ?
　　_____
　　_____

8　restaurants / How / many / there / in / Indian / are / the / UK ?
　　_____
　　_____

b Match questions 1–8 in exercise a with answers a–h.

a　Only about six grams a day.　　　　　　　⬚ 5
b　Most cheese is about 40 percent fat.　　⬚
c　I have chicken, lamb or beef every day.　⬚
d　About 10,000. There are 1,000 in London.　⬚
e　There isn't much – I think we need some more.　⬚
f　There are a lot of potatoes, but there aren't any carrots.　⬚
g　Three.　⬚
h　One small cup, please.　⬚

c 🎧 **6.7** Listen and check.

12a Complete the questions with *much* or *many*.

1　How _many_ stars are there on the Australian flag?
2　How _____ skin does the average person have?
3　How _____ food does an adult elephant eat each day?
4　How _____ people use Atlanta Airport, USA, every day?
5　How _____ brothers has Prince William got?
6　How _____ water is there in the Sea of Crisis?
7　How _____ people live in Japan?
8　How _____ cars are there in the world?
9　How _____ cheese does the average French person eat each year?
10　How _____ stations are there on the Moscow Metro?

b Choose the correct answer, a or b, for questions 1–10 in exercise a.

1 ⓐ 6	**b** 50
2 **a** 1.5–2 m²	**b** 2–3 m²
3 **a** 35 kilos	**b** 135 kilos
4 **a** 25,200	**b** 252,000
5 **a** 1	**b** 2
6 **a** A lot!	**b** There isn't any.
7 **a** about 127 million	**b** about 230 million
8 **a** over 1 billion	**b** over 2 billion
9 **a** 4 kilos	**b** 24 kilos
10 **a** 186	**b** 313

c 🎧 **6.8** Listen and check.

Writing
Describe a favourite place to eat

13a Read the restaurant review on the website and answer the questions.

1 Where is the restaurant?
2 What kind of food can you eat?

New Garden Chinese restaurant

★★★★⯪

5 people found this review helpful.

Was this review helpful?
<u>YES</u> / <u>NO</u>

My favourite place to eat is New Garden Chinese restaurant. It's in the city centre, inside the shopping centre. The food is very good and it isn't very expensive. I like the sweet and sour chicken. The restaurant serves food to eat in or take away. It's very busy in the evening, so I go there at lunchtime on weekdays.

b Write a review of a restaurant in your town for the website. Use some of the words and phrases in the box.

....

famous for   lively atmosphere   special offer
busy   service   friendly   efficient
a good place to go   my favourite place to eat
at lunchtime   in the evening   flavour
typical dish

....

We have reviews of thousands of restaurants around the world.

What do you want to do?

<u>Read a review</u>.   <u>Write a review</u>.

_____
_____
_____
_____
_____
_____
_____
_____
_____
_____

Language live
Ordering food and drink

14a Choose the correct answers.

1 Can I *eat* / (*have*) one of those, please?
2 Hello, *I like* / *I'd like* a coffee, please.
3 Eat-in or *takeaway* / *go away*?
4 OK. *That's* / *This is* £1.85, please.
5 Nine euros twenty? Here's ten euros. Keep the *money* / *change*.
6 OK. Would you like *anything* / *anyone* else?

b Look at sentences 1–6 in exercise a. Who says these things in a café: the customer or the assistant?

1 *customer*
2 _____
3 _____
4 _____
5 _____
6 _____

c Complete the conversations with sentences 1–6 in exercise a.

1 **A:** *Can I have one of those, please?*
   B: One of these chocolate cakes? Yes, here you are.
2 **A:** I'd like one cheese sandwich, please.
   B: _____
   A: Eat-in please.
3 **A:** _____
   B: Sure. Cappuccino, filter coffee or espresso?
   A: Espresso, please.
4 **A:** Can I have one banana muffin, please.
   B: _____
5 **A:** Can we have two pizzas, please?
   B: _____
   A: No, thanks.
6 **A:** Right, that's 9 euros 20 cents.
   B: _____
   A: Oh, thanks very much!

d 🎧 **6.9** Listen and check.

15 Write a similar conversation. Use the phrases in exercise 14 and your own ideas.

_____
_____
_____
_____
_____
_____
_____
_____

Grammar focus 1
Past simple: *was/were*

1 Complete the sentences with *was* or *were*.

1 My grandparents __were__ married for more than 50 years.
2 When I _____ in Berlin last year, the weather _____ very cold.
3 How many people _____ there at the party?
4 Where _____ you on Saturday evening?
5 It _____ a beautiful day in August. My family and I _____ on holiday at the seaside.
6 _____ George at school today?
7 How _____ your first day at work?
8 It _____ very nice to meet you, Mr Brown.

2a Read the statements and decide if they are true (T) or false (F). Correct the false statements.

1 In 2012, the Olympic Games were in London. [T]
_____

2 The Berlin Wall was in Russia. [F]
The Berlin Wall wasn't in Russia.
It was in Germany.

3 The winner of the 2012 US election was Mitt Romney. ☐
_____
_____

4 The Beatles were famous in the 1940s. ☐
_____
_____

5 The world football champions in 2010 were Spain. ☐
_____
_____

6 Steve Jobs was the boss of Microsoft. ☐
_____
_____

7 Nelson Mandela was the president of South Africa. ☐
_____
_____

8 Daniel Radcliffe was in the James Bond films. ☐
_____
_____

b 🎧 **7.1 Listen and check.**

3a Read about the famous people below. Complete the questions and write short answers.

Mark Twain
American writer
– born 1835
– died 1910

1 A: _Was_____ Mark Twain a painter?
  B: _No, he wasn't._____
2 A: _Was_____ he American?
  B: _Yes, he was._____

Charlie Chaplin
Film actor
– born London 1889
– died Switzerland 1977

3 A: _____ Charlie Chaplin born in the USA?
  B: _____
4 A: _____ he an actor?
  B: _____

The Marx Brothers
American comedians
– all born in Germany

5 A: _____ the Marx Brothers born in the USA?
  B: _____
6 A: _____ they comedians?
  B: _____

Anna Pavlova
Russian dancer
– died 1931

7 A: _____ Anna Pavlova Russian?
   B: _____

8 A: _____ she a singer?
   B: _____

Pelé and Jairzinho
Brazilian – the 1970
World Cup team

9 A: _____ Pelé and Jairzinho from Argentina?
   B: _____

10 A: _____ they footballers?
   B: _____

b 🎧 7.2 Listen and check. Practise saying the questions and answers.

4a Complete the conversation with *was/wasn't* (-) or *were/weren't* (+).

A: Hi. Where ¹ _was_ (+) you yesterday?

B: I ² _was_ (+) in the library.
A: What? No, you ³ _weren't_ (–) in the library!
B: Yes, I ⁴_____ (+).
A: Well, I didn't see you. I ⁵_____ (+) there all day from eight to five.
B: No, that's not true. The library doesn't open at eight o'clock. It opens at nine o'clock every day.
A: Oh yes, you're right. I ⁶_____ (+) there from nine to five.
B: Really? Well, I ⁷_____ (+) there at one o'clock. And you ⁸_____ (–) there!
A: Oh yes, that's right, too. I ⁹_____ (–) in the library then. I ¹⁰_____ (+) in town.
B: Who ¹¹_____ (+) you in town with?
A: I ¹²_____ (+) with Roberto. We went for lunch. Then I ¹³_____ (+) in the library again from two to five.
B: Oh right. I ¹⁴_____ (–) there for long. I went home at about half past one.
A: So, where are you now?
B: In the library. Where are you?
A: In bed!

b 🎧 7.3 Listen and check.

5 Look again at the conversation in exercise 4a. Write a similar conversation and add different details.

_____
_____
_____
_____
_____
_____
_____
_____
_____
_____
_____
_____
_____
_____
_____
_____
_____
_____
_____
_____
_____
_____

Listen and read

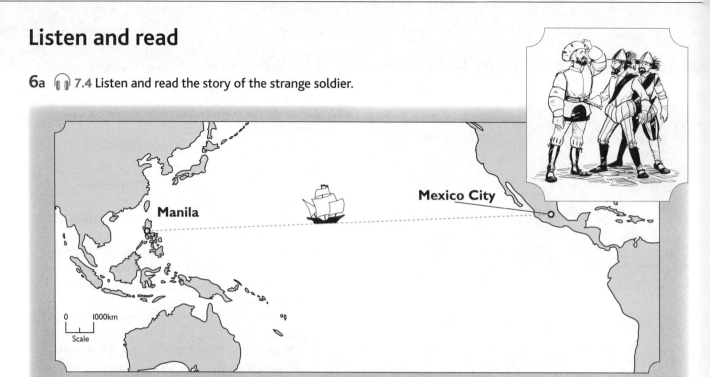

The Strange Soldier

It was a beautiful sunny morning in Mexico City. The date was October 10th, the year was 1593.

In the main square of the city, soldiers stood in front of the Royal Palace. The people of the city came and went as usual. But there was something strange about one of the soldiers: he wore a different uniform from the others. When the other soldiers saw him, they began asking him questions. 'Who are you? Where are you from?' one of the other soldiers asked. 'I am a Spanish soldier,' he answered, 'and because the governor died last night, it is my job to stay in front of the palace here.' 'The governor?' one of the soldiers replied, 'Which governor?' 'The governor of Manila, of course.'

The other soldiers told him he was in Mexico City – thousands of kilometres from the city of Manila. The young soldier was amazed and had no idea how he came to be in a city so far from his home.

Nobody believed his strange story. In the end, they put the young man in prison, and left him there until they decided what to do.

Two months later, a Spanish ship arrived from Manila. It brought news that the governor of Manila was dead – and the time of his death was 10 p.m. on the evening of October 9th, 1593. Was the young man's story true?

Four hundred years later, no one knows how it was possible for a man to travel across the world in one night … without knowing how or why.

b Read the story again and put the events in the correct order.

a The Mexican soldiers saw the strange soldier. ___

b The governor of Manila died. _1_

c They put the strange soldier in prison. ___

d A ship from Manila arrived in Mexico City. ___

e The strange soldier travelled from Manila to Mexico. ___

Vocabulary
Life events

7 Match 1–5 with a–e to make phrases. Then match 6–11 with f–k.

1 start	d	**a** job
2 study	☐	**b** maths
3 move to	☐	**c** children
4 have	☐	**d** school
5 get a	☐	**e** a different town
6 go	☐	**f** married
7 get	☐	**g** school
8 meet	☐	**h** business
9 leave	☐	**i** someone
10 start a	☐	**j** to university
11 graduate	☐	**k** from university

8 Complete the text with the words in the box.

~~went~~   ~~started~~   studied   met   got (x2)
moved   graduated   started   had

Ruth Lawrence was born in Brighton, England. As a child, she didn't go to school. She had lessons with her father. She was very clever and very, very good at maths, and she [1] _went_ to Oxford University. She [2] _started_ university in 1983, when she was twelve years old. She [3] _____ maths. She [4] _____ from Oxford University after only two years (students usually graduate after three years). Then she [5] _____ a job at Harvard University.

But then she [6] _____ someone and they fell in love. His name was Ari Naimark. Ruth and Ari [7] _____ married and they [8] _____ to Jerusalem. They [9] _____ four children and their first child [10] _____ school in 2006. And what is her husband's job? He's a mathematician, too!

Grammar focus 2
Past simple: regular and irregular verbs

9 Write the Past simple form of the verbs.

1 like   _liked_
2 enjoy   _____
3 travel   _____
4 study   _____
5 look   _____
6 dance   _____
7 play   _____
8 believe   _____
9 arrive   _____
10 try   _____
11 receive   _____
12 stay   _____

10 Complete the sentences with the Past simple form of the verbs in the box.

~~graduate~~   study   change   try   start
die   work   end   live   help   walk

1 My brother _graduated_ last year. He was at Glasgow University.
2 The Second World War _____ in 1939 and _____ six years later, in 1945.
3 Elvis Presley, the king of rock'n'roll, _____ in 1977.
4 There were no more buses, so I _____ home.
5 When I was at school, my parents often _____ me with my homework.
6 I _____ French when I was at school, but I don't remember very much now.
7 I _____ to phone you last night, but there was no answer.
8 When he was a young musician, Reg Dwight _____ his name to Elton John.
9 I _____ in finance for a big computer company from 2001 to 2011.
10 The composer Chopin was born in Poland, but he _____ in France for many years.

11 Complete the sentences with the Past simple form of the verb in brackets.

Three child stars of the past

Mozart …
- [1] _wrote_ (write) music when he was five years old.
- [2] _____ (leave) home when he was only 12 years old.
- [3] _____ (go) to live in Vienna when he was 25 years old.

Shirley Temple …
- [4] _____ (make) her first film when she was six.
- [5] _____ (win) an Oscar in 1934.
- [6] _____ (become) a politician in the 1970s.

Michael Jackson …
- [7] _____ (begin) singing at the age of five.
- [8] _____ (sing) with his four brothers in the Jackson Five.
- [9] _____ (sell) millions of records before he was 18.

12 Complete the sentences with the Past simple form of the verb in brackets.

1 Martin Scorsese __made__ (make) the film *Hugo*.
2 Lindsay's holiday last year _____ (cost) over 2,000 euros.
3 Lucy's parents _____ (give) her a car for her 21st birthday.
4 We were both so hot and thirsty that we _____ (drink) two bottles of mineral water.
5 Steve _____ (become) a writer when he was 45.
6 Karen's got a fantastic job – last month she _____ (earn) 8,000 euros!
7 The police looked everywhere for the money, but they only _____ (find) an empty bag.
8 Jan and Anna _____ (fall) in love with each other at my birthday party two years ago.
9 The first Spiderman film _____ (come out) in 2002.
10 Last year we _____ (go) to the cinema a lot.

13a Complete the text with the Past simple form of the verbs in brackets.

Seventy years ago, Amelia Earhart [1] __was__ (be) America's favourite woman. In 1932, she [2] _____ (fly) across the Atlantic Ocean alone – the first woman to do this.

Her journey [3] _____ (start) in Newfoundland, Canada: fifteen hours later, her Lockheed Vega aeroplane [4] _____ (arrive) in Londonderry, Northern Ireland. People all over the world [5] _____ (want) to meet this incredible woman. She [6] _____ (meet) King George V of England and [7] _____ (become) friends with the US President Franklin D. Roosevelt. The American people [8] _____ (love) her.

Five years later, Amelia [9] _____ (try) to fly around the world. An American University [10] _____ (give) her $50,000 for a new Lockheed Electra aeroplane. On the morning of July 2nd 1937, Amelia and her co-pilot, Fred Noonan, [11] _____ (leave) Lae in New Guinea and [12] _____ (begin) their journey to Howland Island in the Pacific Ocean.

On July 3rd 1937, the American ship *Itasca* [13] _____ (receive) a radio message from Amelia. A few minutes later her plane [14] _____ (disappear). American ships [15] _____ (spend) nearly two weeks looking for the plane, but they [16] _____ (find) nothing.

b 🎧 **7.5 Listen and check.**

Pronunciation
Regular Past simple forms

14a Say the words and count the syllables.

1	started	_2_	7	needed	___
2	walked	_1_	8	liked	___
3	loved	___	9	died	___
4	wanted	___	10	waited	___
5	moved	___	11	lived	___
6	worked	___	12	checked	___

b 🎧 **7.6 Listen and check.**

Vocabulary
Past time phrases

15 Complete the sentences with the words in the box.

~~weekend~~	this	ago	last
years	Tuesday	when	was

1 What did you do last __weekend__ ?
2 My brother got married _____ he was 20 years old.
3 I went shopping _____ morning.
4 The film started ten minutes _____ .
5 Did you have a party on your birthday _____ year?
6 My grandfather died four _____ ago.
7 I saw a good film on _____ .
8 I graduated from university when I _____ 21 years old.

16 Complete the sentences with the words in the box.

~~in~~	at	from	to	on	in (x3)	ago

1 The economic situation in our country became much better __in__ the 2000s.
2 The café is open _____ 8:30 in the morning _____ about eleven o'clock in the evening.
3 Vanessa started dancing lessons four years _____ .
4 We decided to have our holidays _____ September, when it's not so hot.
5 _____ the age of seven, Vanessa started dancing lessons.
6 I stayed at home _____ Friday because I had so much work to do.
7 I was born _____ 1993.
8 There was a war between the two countries _____ the 19th century.

Vocabulary
Adjectives to describe stories

1 Match the types of story in the box with pictures 1–5.

romance   science fiction   action
historical   comedy

1 *romance*

2 _____

3 _____

4 _____

5 _____

2 Find 10 more adjectives to describe stories in the word square.

F	U	F	D	B	R	O	Y	E	A	I	L
S	E	R	I	O	U	S	H	A	N	P	R
L	N	I	E	R	O	M	A	N	T	I	C
O	I	G	R	I	R	G	P	I	T	E	P
W	G	H	T	N	T	D	P	L	Y	E	V
E	F	T	O	G	Y	B	Y	M	K	X	H
X	B	E	I	L	E	S	W	T	U	C	J
E	E	N	J	O	Y	A	B	L	E	I	B
N	U	I	Y	G	N	D	L	O	R	T	C
F	U	N	N	Y	V	H	Q	N	M	I	W
N	A	G	I	D	X	S	I	G	Y	N	A
O	F	A	S	T	M	O	V	I	N	G	L

Grammar focus 1
Past simple: negative form

3 Complete the sentences with the negative form of the verb.

1 You ate the chicken, but you ___didn't eat___ the chips.
2 I enjoyed the acting in the film, but I _____ the songs.
3 We visited the castle, but we _____ the museum.
4 I studied science at school, but I _____ history.
5 They had something to drink, but they _____ anything to eat.
6 She downloaded some music, but she _____ the film.
7 He talked about his job, but he _____ about his family.
8 I liked him, but I _____ his wife.

4 Make the sentences negative.

1 We had good weather when we were on holiday.
   We didn't have good weather when we were on holiday.
2 We went for a drive yesterday.
   _____
3 Ben remembered to buy a birthday card.
   _____
4 I heard the phone.
   _____
5 I checked my email yesterday.
   _____
6 I ate in a restaurant last night.
   _____
7 Amanda knew what to do.
   _____
8 The letter arrived this morning.
   _____

5 Find and correct the mistakes in six of the sentences.

1 We didn't went to the theatre at the weekend. ☐
   We didn't go to the theatre at the weekend.
2 I didn't speak English when I was a child. ☑
   _____
3 I went to their house, but they wasn't at home. ☐
   _____
4 We didn't see the concert because they didn't have any tickets. ☐
   _____
5 I didn't finish my homework because I didn't had time. ☐
   _____
6 The wallet wasn't very expensive, but I didn't like it, so I didn't buy it. ☐
   _____
7 It wasn't a good story and we weren't interested in it. ☐
   _____
8 We weren't go out last night. ☐
   _____
9 The film didn't be very good, so I didn't watch it all. ☐
   _____
10 I didn't met my grandmother in the city yesterday. ☐
   _____

Vocabulary
Entertainment

6 There is one mistake in every line in the text. Add *to*, *for* or *a* in the correct places.

> I had a great weekend. On Friday, I cooked dinner ^*for* some friends.
>
> After dinner, we went ^*to* a musical. It was really funny.
>
> I came back at about 11 p.m. and watched DVD at home.
>
> On Saturday, I got up late. It was a nice day, so I went a walk.
>
> Then my friend phoned and said, 'Do you want to go a party tonight?'
>
> I said, 'Great! Let's go out dinner first.' We had a great evening.
>
> On Sunday, I wanted to do something – maybe go the theatre
>
> or perhaps go the cinema. But I was very tired, so I didn't go out.
>
> I just stayed at home and read book. Sometimes you need to rest!

Grammar focus 2

Past simple: question form

7a Use the prompts to write questions about famous people from the past.

1 Shakespeare / write / *Romeo and Juliet*?
   Did Shakespeare write 'Romeo and Juliet'?

2 Alexander Graham Bell / invent / email?
   _____

3 Marilyn Monroe / sing / *Candle in the Wind*?
   _____

4 Captain Cook / discover / America?
   _____

5 Leonardo da Vinci / paint / the *Mona Lisa*?
   _____

6 Madonna / play / Evita?
   _____

7 Beethoven / write / rock songs?
   _____

8 Laurel and Hardy / make / comedy films?
   _____

9 Yuri Gagarin / travel / to the moon?
   _____

b Write short answers for the questions in exercise a.

1 *Yes, he did.* _____
2 _____
3 _____
4 _____
5 _____
6 _____
7 _____
8 _____
9 _____

c 🎧 **8.1** Listen and check. Practise saying the questions and answers.

8a Look at the papers from Simon's business trip and write questions about his trip.

Ticket Reservation EUROSTAR STANDARD

London St Pancras – Paris Nord (single)		
Departure:	Time: 2:30 p.m.	Date: 23/08
Journey time:	2 hours 16 minutes	
Price:	£125.00	

THE STATION BUFFET RESTAURANT
PHONE: 020 734534554

1 set menu   £14.50
+ Service (10%)
Total: £15.95

The Station Bookshop
London
23/08 13:58
Blue Guide to France   9.99
English—French Dictionary   4.99
                    Total   14.98

1 **A:** _Where did he_ go?
  B: He went to Paris.

2 **A:** _____ travel?
  B: By train.

3 **A:** _____ have lunch?
  B: At The Station Buffet Restaurant.

4 **A:** _____ cost?
  B: £15.95.

5 **A:** _____ at the station?
  B: Some books.

6 **A:** _____ buy?
  B: Two.

7 **A:** _____ leave?
  B: At 2:30.

8 **A:** _____ take?
  B: Two hours and sixteen minutes.

b 🎧 **8.2** Listen and check. Practise saying the questions and answers.

9 Find and correct the mistakes in the sentences.

1 Did you had a nice weekend?
Did you have a nice weekend?

2 'Did you see Alistair at the party?' 'Yes, I saw.'
_____

3 Did you bought a newspaper yesterday?
_____
_____

4 You listen to the news last night?
_____
_____

5 'Did you like the concert?' 'No, I didn't like.'
_____
_____

6 Did you lived in Poland when you were 13?
_____
_____

7 You use my computer this afternoon?
_____
_____

8 Do you listen to your parents when you were young?
_____
_____

Pronunciation
Linking

10a 🎧 **8.3** Listen to the questions. Notice the linking in some of the questions between *did* and *you/your*.

1 Did it rain yesterday?
2 Did you get wet?
3 What did you see at the cinema?
4 How much did your ticket cost?
5 What time did the film start?
6 When did it finish?
7 Did your friends like it?
8 What did you all do after the film?

b Listen again. Practise saying the questions.

Listen and read

11a 🎧 **8.4** Read and listen to the text about a hero and heroine.

National heroes

Mustafa Kemal Atatürk

Mustafa Kemal Atatürk is the father of modern Turkey. He was born in 1881. He chose the army as a career and in 1915, during the First World War, he led the Turkish army at Gelibolu and Istanbul. By the end of the war, he was a hero and from that time on, all of the Turkish people supported him. He led the Turkish army in the War of Independence (1919–1922) and in 1923, he became the first president of the new Republic of Turkey. During the last 15 years of his life, Atatürk introduced many reforms and did many things to improve life in Turkey. He died in November 1938, but today the people of Turkey still think of him with great respect.

and heroines

Florence Nightingale

A hundred and fifty years ago, most nurses did not study nursing. But a British woman called Florence Nightingale tried to change all that. In the 1850s, she worked in a hospital for wounded soldiers in the Crimea (now Ukraine). People say she never slept, but spent all her time helping the men. The soldiers called her 'The Lady of the Lamp' because of the lamp she always carried as she walked around at night. When she returned to England, she began a school of nursing in London. She died in 1910.

Glossary: Gelibolu = Gallipoli; wounded = hurt in a battle or war

b Read the text again and write questions for the answers.

1 A: *When was Mustafa Kemal Atatürk born?*
   B: In 1881.

2 A: _____
   B: He led the Turkish army at Gelibolu and Istanbul.

3 A: _____
   B: In 1923.

4 A: _____
   B: In 1938.

5 A: _____
   B: In the 1850s.

6 A: _____
   B: 'The Lady of the Lamp'.

7 A: _____
   B: When she returned to England.

Language live
Arranging an evening out

12 Complete the conversations with the words in the box.

~~free~~   want   Sounds   like
busy   time   idea   How

1 A: Are you _free_ on Friday?
   B: Sorry, I'm _____ then, but I'm not doing anything on Saturday.

2 A: Do you _____ to go out for a pizza?
   B: Good _____ . I'm really hungry!

3 A: _____ about an evening out tomorrow?
   B: Why not? _____ good – let's go to a nightclub.

4 A: Would you _____ to go to the cinema on Saturday afternoon?
   B: No, thanks. Maybe another _____ ?

13 Write a similar conversation. Use the phrases in exercise 12 and your own ideas.

_____
_____
_____

Writing
Arranging an evening out

14a Complete the message with the words in the box.

~~everyone~~   next   It's   meeting
celebrate   See   let's   evening

> **Profile** | **Info** | **Messages**
>
> Hi, [1]_everyone_ !
> [2]_____ my birthday on Thursday
> [3]_____ week, so let's have an [4]_____ out
> to [5]_____ . I want to go to Pasta Express, so
> [6]_____ meet there.
> The [7]_____ time is 7:30. [8]_____
> you there!
>
> Helen xxx

b 🎧 **8.5** Listen and check.

c Write a message to your friends to arrange an evening out in your town.

> **Profile** | **Info** | **Messages**
>
> _____
> _____
> _____
> _____
> _____
> _____
> _____

Vocabulary
Describing objects

1 Complete the sentences with a suitable word. The first letter of each word is given.

1 My brother stayed in a very e<u>xpensive</u> hotel. It was 6,000 euros a night!
2 But my sister stayed in a very c_____ hostel. It was only 15 euros a night.
3 My mum gave me an o_____ leather jacket. She bought it in 1970!
4 She was wearing u_____ shoes, so she took them off on the way home.
5 Claire's got a very p_____ dress. It's got red and blue flowers on it and it looks lovely.
6 The plane's really f_____ – it does the journey in just 25 minutes.
7 My washing machine's very e_____ . It doesn't use much electricity, so it's cheap to use.
8 Everyone wore glasses like that 15 years ago, but they are not very f_____ now.

2 Complete the conversations with the words in the box.

....
~~uncomfortable~~   easy to use   powerful
economical   unusual   stylish
....

1 **A:** Does that chair feel nice when you're sitting on it?
  B: No, it's very <u>uncomfortable</u> .
2 **A:** Small cars don't use very much petrol.
  B: Yes, they're very _____ . They can save you money.
3 **A:** People in Milan have really fashionable clothes. And all the shops look beautiful.
  B: Yes, it's a very _____ city.
4 **A:** I only bought a new mobile this morning and I can already use it with no problems.
  B: Yes, it's very _____ .
5 **A:** Is it true that racing cars can go from 0 to 200 km per hour in four seconds?
  B: Yes, they're very _____ cars.
6 **A:** Look! I've never seen a hat like that!
  B: Oh yes, it's _____ . But it's not very stylish.

Grammar focus 1
Comparative adjectives

3 Add letters to make the comparative form of the adjectives.

1 young _e r_
2 eas _ _ _
3 big _ _ _
4 cheap _ _
5 health _ _ _
6 new _ _
7 happ _ _ _
8 slim _ _ _
9 quiet _ _
10 hot _ _ _

4 Use the prompts to make sentences. Use the comparative form of the adjectives.

1 My mum / old / my dad
  My mum is older than my dad.
2 Tea / cheap / coffee
  _____
3 My new car / economical / my old car
  _____
4 Janina / fashionable / Sara
  _____
5 Her jewellery / pretty / her dress
  _____
6 Castle Hotel / expensive / Beach View Hotel
  _____
7 The shower in the hotel / powerful / the shower at home
  _____
8 The new software / easy to use / the old software
  _____
9 Tokyo in Japan / busy / Pisa in Italy
  _____
10 My sister / tall / me
  _____

5a Read the two facts, then write a sentence using the comparative form of the adjectives in brackets.

1 The area of Brazil is 8.5 million km².
   The area of Australia is 7.6 million km².
   Brazil is bigger than Australia. _____ (big)

2 The Volga River in Russia is 3,600 km long.
   The Mississippi River in the USA is 6,000 km long.
   _____ (long)

3 Blue whales usually weigh about 130 tonnes.
   Elephants usually weigh about 7 tonnes.
   _____ (heavy)

4 The Pyramids in Egypt are about 4,000 years old.
   The Parthenon in Greece is about 2,500 years old.
   _____ (old)

5 The Eiffel Tower in Paris is 324 m tall.
   The Burj Khalifa in Dubai is 828 m tall.
   _____ (tall)

6 The Akashi-Kaikyo Bridge in Japan is 1,991 m long.
   The Sydney Harbour Bridge in Australia is 503 m long.
   _____ (long)

7 The price of gold is about $50,000 per kilo.
   The price of silver is about $1,000 per kilo.
   _____ (expensive)

8 English has more than a hundred irregular verbs.
   Esperanto has no irregular verbs!
   _____ (easy)

b 🎧 9.1 Listen and check. Practise saying the sentences.

6 Find and correct the mistakes in five of the sentences.

1 Delhi is bigger than Bangalore. ☑
_____

2 Maths is easier that science. ☐
   Maths is easier than science.

3 A sports car is powerful than a scooter. ☐
_____

4 The film was more interesting than the book. ☐
_____

5 Ben's clothes are more stylish Harry's clothes. ☐
_____

6 Pasta Express is expensive more than The Thai Place. ☐
_____

7 The weather in January is worse than the weather in June. ☐
_____

8 My new bed is uncomfortable than my old bed. ☐
_____

Pronunciation
Stressed syllables

7a 🎧 9.2 Listen to the sentences. Notice the stressed syllables.

1 My phone was expensive.
2 But my watch was more expensive.
3 I'm nice.
4 But you're nicer!
5 The film was good.
6 But the book was better.
7 I'm not very fashionable.
8 But my sister is more fashionable than me.
9 Flying there isn't economical.
10 It's more economical to go by train.

b Listen again. Practise saying the sentences.

Grammar focus 2
Superlative adjectives

8 Read the information about the Olympic athletes and complete the sentences. Use the superlative form of the adjective in brackets.

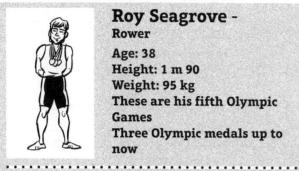

Roy Seagrove -
Rower

Age: 38
Height: 1 m 90
Weight: 95 kg
These are his fifth Olympic Games
Three Olympic medals up to now

Jim Bowen -
Basketball player

Age: 19
Height: 1 m 95
Weight: 89 kg
First Olympic Games
Started playing basketball three months ago

Jake Kay -
Marathon runner

Age: 25
Height: 1 m 60
Weight: 51 kg
Silver medal in the last Olympics

Karina Green -
Swimmer

Age: 16
Height: 1 m 72
Weight: 57 kg
First Olympic Games

1 _Roy Seagrove_ is _the oldest_ . (old)
2 _____ is _____ . (young)
3 _____ has got _____ hair. (long)
4 _____ has got _____ hair. (short)
5 _____ is _____ . (tall)
6 _____ is _____ . (heavy)
7 _____ is _____ . (small)
8 _____ is _____ . (successful)

9a Complete the questions with the superlative form of the adjective in brackets.

Approximate average distance from the Sun

SOLARSYSTEM

		Distance from Sun	Average temperature
1	Mercury	57 million km	−173–427°C
2	Venus	108 million km	462°C
3	Earth	150 million km	15°C
4	Mars	228 million km	−63°C
5	Jupiter	778 million km	−148°C
6	Saturn	1.4 billion km	178°C
7	Uranus	2.9 billion km	−216°C
8	Neptune	4.5 billion km	−214°C

1 Which is _the nearest_ (near) planet to the Sun?
2 What's the _____ (small) planet?
3 This planet has got over 30 moons and it's _____ (big) planet in the solar system.
4 Which is _____ (hot) planet?
5 This is the _____ (far) planet from the Sun.
6 Which planet is _____ (near) to Uranus?
7 Which planet is _____ (close) to Earth?
8 Which is _____ (cold) planet?

b Look at the questions and picture in exercise a again. Can you answer the questions?

1 _Mercury_
2 _____
3 _____
4 _____
5 _____
6 _____
7 _____
8 _____

10a Complete the joke with the comparative or superlative form of the adjective in brackets.

A woman went into ¹*the most expensive* (expensive) butcher's in town and asked for ² _____ (big) chicken in the shop. The shopkeeper showed her a chicken and said 'This is ³ _____ (good) chicken in the shop, madam.' 'It's very small,' she said. 'Have you got a ⁴ _____ (large) one?' 'Just a moment,' said the shopkeeper. He took the chicken into another room. In fact, it was the only chicken he had. So he put some sausages inside to make it look ⁵ _____ (big).

'Here you are,' he said. 'This is our ⁶ _____ (delicious) chicken. And you can see that it's ⁷ _____ (big) than the other. But I'm afraid it's also ⁸ _____ (expensive).'

'Hmm ... but I'm not sure if it's ⁹ _____ (good) than the other. OK. Can I have both of them, please?'

b 🎧 **9.3** Listen and check.

Vocabulary
Shops and services

11a Put the letters in brackets in the correct order to make the names of shops.

1 You can buy steak at a ___*butcher's*___ . (brushtec')
2 You can buy shirts, trousers and skirts at a _____ . (loshcet posh)
3 You can buy bread at a _____ . (akbers')
4 You can buy stamps and send parcels at a _____ . (stop coffei)
5 You can buy medicine at a _____ . (harmycap)
6 You can have a haircut at a _____ . (sderrahisser')
7 You can buy a present at a _____ . (figt ohps)
8 You can take your clothes for cleaning at a _____ . (ryd sercanel')

b 🎧 **9.4** Listen and check. Practise saying the sentences.

12 Complete the conversations with the words in the box.

estate agent's	optician's	baker's
post office	butcher's	pharmacy
hairdresser's	dry-cleaner's	

1 **A:** Jane, how did you find your flat? Did you look online?
 B: No, I went to an _*estate agent's*_ . He told me about the flat and I went to see it. And now I'm living there.
2 **A:** I need to buy some medicine and a new toothbrush. Is there a _____ near here?
 B: Yes, it's there, next to the gift shop.
3 **A:** Oh no! I've got chocolate on my coat – it looks horrible!
 B: Don't worry. There's a very good _____ in town. They'll clean it for you.
4 **A:** I couldn't make a cake. I didn't have time!
 B: Oh dear! Let's go to the _____ and buy one.
5 **A:** Are you going to the _____ ?
 B: Yes, I am.
 A: Oh good, can you get me some stamps?
6 **A:** Your hair's really long. Why don't you go to the _____ ?
 B: No. I'm going to cut it myself!
7 **A:** Have we got anything for supper tonight?
 B: No, but I can get a chicken from the _____ .
8 **A:** I'm worried about my eyes. I can't see very well.
 B: Why don't you go to the _____ ?

Listen and read

13a 🎧 **9.5** Listen and read the text about three machines you can buy to make your life easier.

THE THREE MOST INTELLIGENT MACHINES FOR YOUR HOME

Thanks to computer chips, you can now buy machines that can think!!
Here are some of the best machines which can really make your life easier.

THE SMOOTHLINE D838 ROBOT VACUUM CLEANER

Do you like housework? No? Then this new robot vacuum cleaner is the machine for you. It can clean your living room automatically. It has a computer which tells it to go around objects such as chairs and table legs as it cleans your floor. And if a person – or your pet dog or cat – comes too close, it stops automatically.

The Smoothline D838 Robot Vacuum Cleaner costs £1,800.

THE FZ SMART FRIDGE

A fridge which tells you what it's got inside and gives you ideas about what to cook for dinner! A visual display shows you what's inside the fridge – you don't even have to open the door; and the fridge can also tell when food is too old to use. And if you haven't got any ideas about what to cook for your family this evening, just touch the computer screen on the door of the fridge and you can look at over a thousand of your favourite recipes. You can also use it to send emails and to surf the internet!

The FZ Smart Fridge is more than just a fridge and costs only £999!

THE ULTIMATE POWER CONTROL SYSTEM

How many remote control units do you have in your house – for the TV, the DVD player, home audio? Now you can control everything in your house – from a light in the bedroom to your front door – using just one special remote control unit. It works with radio signals, so you can do everything in your house without getting out of bed. You can even surf the internet, send emails, watch videos or listen to music with the Ultimate Power Control System's video screen.

The Ultimate Power Control System costs £45.

b Read the text again and answer the questions.

1 Which machine is the most useful?

The Smoothline D838 Robot Vacuum Cleaner.

2 Which machine is the cheapest?

_____

3 Which machine is the most useful for cooking ideas?

_____

4 Which machine is the most expensive?

_____

5 Which machine is the smallest?

_____

6 Which machine is the best one for people who hate housework?

_____

Vocabulary
Clothes

1a Add letters to complete the types of clothes.

1 s <u>u</u> <u>i</u> t   <u>b, c</u>
2 t _ _   <u>b</u>
3 sk _ rt   ____
4 b _ s _ b _ ll c _ p ____
5 tr _ _ s _ r s   ____
6 tr _ _ n _ r s   ____
7 sh _ r t   ____
8 s _ ngl _ ss _ s   ____
9 j _ ck _ t   ____
10 j _ mp _ r   ____
11 dr _ ss   ____

b Where do you wear the clothes in exercise a? Write a–d next to 1–11.

a on your head
b on your upper body
c on your legs
d on your feet

2 Look at Bob, Paul and Marie. Who is wearing the clothes below?

1 trainers   <u>Bob</u>
2 a skirt   _____
3 a tie   _____
4 a shirt   _____
5 jeans   _____
6 a suit   _____
7 trousers   _____
8 a white jacket _____
9 a jumper   _____

Bob

Paul

Marie

Pronunciation
Clothes

3a 🎧 10.1 Listen to the words in the box. Practise saying them.

1 tie ☐
2 baseball cap ☐
3 shirt ☐
4 sunglasses ☐
5 jacket ☐
6 jumper ☐
7 skirt ☑
8 dress ☐
9 jeans ☐
10 shorts ☐
11 trousers ☐
12 trainers ☐

b 🎧 10.2 Listen to Ellie talking about what she is wearing. Tick (✓) the clothes from exercise a you hear.

Grammar focus 1
Present continuous

4 Write the *-ing* form of the verbs.

1 read   <u>reading</u>
2 study   _____
3 wash   _____
4 leave   _____
5 come   _____
6 stop   _____
7 look   _____
8 dance _____
9 stay   _____
10 give   _____
11 plan   _____
12 write _____

5a Look at the picture and complete the sentences. Use the present continuous form of the verb in brackets.

1 The robot _is cleaning_ (clean) the living room.
2 Veronica _____ (look) out of the window.
3 She _____ (talk) to someone on her mobile phone.
4 The baby _____ (sit) on the floor.
5 The baby _____ (eat) the flowers.
6 Ronald _____ (have) a cup of tea.
7 He _____ (watch) television.
8 The two older children _____ (do) their homework.

b 🎧 **10.3** Listen and check. Practise saying the sentences.

6a Complete the questions with question words.

1 _What_ are you doing?
2 _____ are you going?
3 _____ are you smiling?
4 _____ are you talking to?
5 _____ are you reading?
6 _____ are you watching?

b Match questions 1–6 in exercise a with answers a–f.

a Because you look so funny! [3]
b My brother. ☐
c Oh, nothing, just a magazine. ☐
d To my English class. ☐
e Sh! It's my favourite programme. ☐
f My homework. ☐

c 🎧 **10.4** Listen and check. Practise saying the questions and answers.

7 Write short answers to the questions.

1 **A:** Are you enjoying the party, Jo?
   B: Yes, _____I am_____ .
2 **A:** Is it raining outside?
   B: No, _____ .
3 **A:** Are your friends staying in this hotel?
   B: Yes, _____ .
4 **A:** Are you two coming with us?
   B: Yes, _____ .
5 **A:** Are you waiting to see the doctor?
   B: No, _____ .
6 **A:** Is Thomas driving?
   B: Yes, _____ .
7 **A:** Is she talking to us?
   B: No, _____ .

8a Complete the conversation with the Present continuous form of the verb in brackets.

S = Sophie **J** = Jenny
S: It's me, Sophie.
J: Hi, Sophie. Where are you? What ¹_are you doing_ (you / do)?
S: I'm at my sister's wedding.
J: Fantastic! ²_____ (you / enjoy) yourself?
S: No, ³_____ ! I ⁴_____ (not have) a good time. It's awful!
J: Why? What ⁵_____ (happen)?
S: Well, there's the music, for a start. They ⁶_____ (play) this awful 80s music and ... oh no, I don't believe it! My dad ⁷_____ (dance) with my mum's sister!
J: How about your mum? ⁸_____ (she / dance), too?
S: No, ⁹_____ . She ¹⁰_____ (not do) anything. She ¹¹_____ (look) at my dad.
J: Oh dear!
S: Just a minute ... There's a very good-looking young man over there. There's a girl talking to him but he ¹²_____ (not listen) and ... oh!
J: Sophie, what ¹³_____ (he / do)?
S: He ¹⁴_____ (come over)! Talk to you later. Bye!

b 🎧 **10.5** Listen and check.

Listen and read

9a 🎧 **10.6** Listen and read the text about street style.

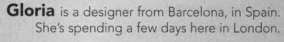

Street Style
Latest Fashion
Blog | News | Celeb Gossip | Contact
51

This week we went to South Molton Street to find out what young people are wearing when they go shopping.

Mina is from London:
She's a student at the London College of Fashion.

'I'm wearing a pair of jeans from Michiko – it's a Japanese shop here in London.'
'I love Japanese clothes! The jumper is from Space, and I bought the jacket at Camden Market a couple of weeks ago. My bag and shoes were presents from my family. I like wearing clothes that are different, so I don't usually go shopping in big shops.'

Gloria is a designer from Barcelona, in Spain. She's spending a few days here in London.

'Because I'm a designer, I love making clothes for myself. I made this dress and the jacket, too! My sunglasses are from Spain, too. They're my favourite sunglasses, but I can't remember where I bought them! I'm looking for a bag which looks good with these clothes. I love shopping in London, but it's very expensive!'

Alice is from the United States. She works for an airline company.

'I travel a lot because of my job. I love my work because I can go shopping in lots of wonderful places. I bought this shirt in Milan and my trousers and shoes are from New York. As well as Italy and the United States, I love shopping here in London, too. I'm going to a shop called Puzzle – it's near here – to buy myself a new jacket.'

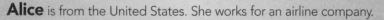

b Read the text again and answer the questions.

1 Where is Mina from?
She's from London.

2 What clothes does Mina talk about?

3 Where is Gloria from?

4 What is Gloria's job?

5 What clothes does Gloria talk about?

6 Where is Alice from?

7 What clothes does Alice talk about?

8 Where did Alice buy her clothes?

Grammar focus 2
Present simple or continuous?

10 Choose the correct answers.

1 Ms Parsons is not in the office today. **She works /
She's working** at home today.

2 'Where **do you come / are you coming** from?'
'I'm Italian – from Milan.'

3 '**Do you speak / Are you speaking** Japanese?'
'Just a little.'

4 Don't forget your umbrella. **It's raining /
It rains** again.

5 'Can you help me with the dinner?' 'Not now.
I watch / I'm watching TV.'

6 In Great Britain, people **drive / are driving** on the left.

7 'Hi! What **do you do / are you doing** here?'
'**I'm waiting / I wait** for a friend.'

8 Can I look at the newspaper now? **Are you
reading / Do you read** it?

9 Can I phone you back later? **We're having /
We have** dinner.

Vocabulary
Describing personality

13 Find the adjectives in the box in the word square.

~~confident~~   bossy   cheerful   determined
easy-going   friendly   hard-working
kind   moody   organised   shy   sociable

C	C	F	T	S	Q	E	F	K	S	F
O	D	H	T	H	D	O	R	I	O	T
N	E	A	S	Y	G	O	I	N	G	E
F	T	R	O	D	A	R	E	D	O	O
I	E	D	C	M	D	G	N	F	C	D
D	R	W	I	F	G	A	D	T	S	W
E	M	O	A	S	M	N	L	E	S	N
N	I	R	B	F	O	I	Y	H	L	S
T	N	K	L	B	O	S	S	Y	Y	G
F	E	I	E	E	D	E	O	L	P	L
T	D	N	G	R	Y	D	S	Y	N	Y
E	G	G	C	H	E	E	R	F	U	L

11a Look at the picture and choose the correct answers.

1 In this picture, four women **shop** / **are shopping** in a supermarket.
2 One of the women, Sally, **carries** / **is carrying** a shopping basket.
3 Sally **works** / **is working** in a hairdresser's.
4 In the picture, Sally **does** / **is doing** some shopping.
5 Jo and her friend Maggie **choose** / **are choosing** fruit.
6 Jo **has** / **is having** a baby.
7 The baby **holds** / **is holding** an apple.
8 Maggie and Jo **look** / **are looking** at the baby.
9 Ahmed is the shop manager. He **puts** / **is putting** things on the shelves in the picture.
10 Ahmed **works** / **is working** very long hours.
11 The woman at the front of the picture is Carrie. She **comes** / **is coming** from China.
12 Carrie **studies** / **is studying** business at university.
13 In the picture, she **buys** / **is buying** her lunch.

b 🎧 10.7 Listen and check.

12 Complete the questions with *is*, *are*, *do* or *does*.

1 _____Is_____ the sun shining today?
2 Where __does__ she come from?
3 What book _____ you reading?
4 Why _____ they laughing?
5 _____ you know Bob?
6 Where _____ you live?
7 Why _____ she doing that?
8 Who _____ he live with?

14a Choose the correct answer.

1 A: Dorota's got lots of friends. She goes out a lot and really loves parties.
   B: Yes, I know. She's very **sociable** / **moody**.
2 A: You're always smiling and you're always happy!
   B: Yes, I'm a very **reliable** / **cheerful** person!
3 A: I arrived at work one hour late today.
   B: Oh dear! What did your boss say?
   A: She just said, 'No problem, you're here now, it's OK.'
   B: You're lucky – your boss is really **easy-going** / **hard-working**.
4 A: Sandra writes a list of all the things she has to do.
   B: Yes, she's really **organised** / **shy**. And she never forgets anything!
5 A: Little children are so **sociable** / **bossy**. My nephew's only three, but he tells me what to do all the time.
   B: My son's the same. He says, 'Dad, come here! Dad, sit down!'
6 A: My new neighbours are very **friendly** / **determined**. When I met them for the first time, they invited me for a cup of tea with them.
   B: That's nice.
7 A: Are you worried about the exam tomorrow, Igor?
   B: No, I think exams are easy. I'm very **confident** / **sociable**.

b 🎧 10.8 Listen and check.

Language live
Asking for goods and services

15a Complete the conversations with the words in the box.

~~haircut~~   owe   What   like
How   size   have   please
this   too   suits   That's

At the hairdresser's

1 A: I'd like a _haircut_ , please.
   B: OK. Do you _____ an appointment?
   A: Yes, I do.

2 A: How would you _____ your hair cut?
   B: Not too long and not too short, _____ .

3 A: How much do I _____ you?
   B: _____ a hundred euros, please. How would you like to pay?
   A: By credit card, please.

At a clothes shop

4 A: I tried this on, but it's _____ small. Have you got this in a larger _____ ?
   B: Yes, here you are.

5 A: Look at this! _____ do you think?
   B: It's great. It _____ you.

6 A: I'll take _____ one, please.
   B: OK. _____ would you like to pay?
   A: By credit card, please.

b 🎧 **10.9 Listen and check.**

16 Write a similar conversation. Use the phrases in exercise 15 and your own ideas.

_____
_____
_____
_____
_____
_____
_____
_____
_____
_____
_____
_____
_____
_____

Writing
Describing people

17a Look at the photo and complete the description with the words in the box.

~~good-looking~~   jacket   dark   shirt
casual   thirties

He's quite [1] _good-looking_. I think he's in his early [2]_____ and he's got short, [3]_____ hair and brown eyes. He's standing up and he's wearing [4]_____ clothes. He's wearing a white [5]_____ but he isn't wearing a [6]_____ or a jumper. He hasn't got a bag.

b Which person does the text in exercise a describe?

c Write a description of one of the people in the photo. Use some of the phrases in the box.

She's in her twenties/forties.
He's in his teens/mid thirties.
short/straight/medium length/blonde hair
He/She's standing up/sitting down/holding a ...
He/She's good-looking/slim.
He/She's got curly hair/a ponytail.

_____
_____
_____
_____
_____
_____
_____
_____
_____
_____
_____

Vocabulary
Animals and natural features

1a Use the clues to complete the grid with the animals in the box.

whales	camels	~~donkeys~~	chimpanzees
elephants	horses	dogs	snakes

1 These animals can carry things and people. They are smaller than horses.
2 Some people think these animals are 'a man's best friend'; they can smell very well.
3 These animals live in the desert and can carry things and people.
4 There are two kinds of these very large animals: Indian and African.
5 These are the largest animals in the world.
6 These animals eat bananas with their hands.
7 These animals don't have legs. Some live on land; some live in the sea.
8 People enjoy riding and racing these animals.

Crossword grid:
1 D O N K E Y S

b Look at the grid. What's the mystery animal?

2a Complete the sentences with the words in the box.

~~volcano~~	sea	forest	beach	ocean
lake	desert	river		

1 The world's biggest _volcano_ is in Hawaii. It is over 4,000 m high and it's active, but it isn't very dangerous.
2 A _____ in Siberia has 31,500 km^3 of water and is 1,620 m deep.
3 Brazilians swim, have parties and play football on this _____ in Rio de Janeiro.
4 This _____ is in Africa, is very hot and has over nine million km^2 of sand.
5 This _____ is the largest area of water in the world and is between America, Australia and Asia.
6 Gorillas live among the trees in this _____ in Uganda.
7 The longest _____ in the world goes through Brazil and Peru.
8 This _____ is less than one percent of the size of the Pacific Ocean and is between Europe and Africa.

b Match places a–h with descriptions 1–8.

a The Pacific Ocean ___5___
b The Sahara Desert ___
c Lake Baikal ___
d Bwindi Forest ___
e The River Amazon ___
f The Mauna Loa Volcano ___
g Copacabana Beach ___
h The Mediterranean Sea ___

Listen and read

3 🎧 **11.1 Listen and read the text about the animal world.**

The animal world

We do not know how many species of animal there are, as people are discovering new ones all the time. But most scientists think that there are about ten million different animal species in the world.

Giraffes are the tallest animals on Earth. A large adult male giraffe can be up to six metres tall. Thanks to its long legs and neck, it can eat the leaves from the tops of trees.

The smallest animals are called protozoa, which have only one cell and are so small that we cannot see them without a powerful microscope.

The smallest mammal is Savi's pygmy shrew – it is only six centimetres long, including its tail.

The goliath frog (Rana Goliath) of West Africa can be up to 75 centimetres long and weighs about 3 kilograms. The goliath beetle is probably the world's largest beetle; it weighs more than 100 grams – about the same as two eggs.

The ostrich is the world's largest bird. An adult ostrich is more than 2.5 metres tall, but it cannot fly.

The bee hummingbird is probably the world's smallest bird. It is just five centimetres long and weighs less than two grams. It can stay still in the air by moving its wings 20 to 50 times a second. One of the largest birds which can fly is the South American condor; its wings are three metres from end to end.

There are more than 50 different types of kangaroo in Australia. When it is born, a baby kangaroo is less than 2.5 centimetres long; but an adult kangaroo can grow to more than two metres in height.

In the mid-1860s, there were about 13 million bison living in North America. By the mid-1880s, there were only a few hundred. Today, there are about 500,000 bison in America, living in special parks.

4 Read the text again and answer the questions.

1 About how many animal species are there in the world? _Ten million._

2 How tall can an adult giraffe grow?
_____

3 How long is the smallest mammal, Savi's pygmy shrew? _____

4 How much does a goliath frog weigh?
_____

5 How tall is an adult ostrich?
_____

6 How fast can a bee hummingbird move its wings?
_____

7 How many types of kangaroo are there?
_____

8 How many bison were there in America in the 1860s?_____

9 How many bison were there in America the 1880s?_____

10 How many bison are there in America now?
_____

Vocabulary
Big numbers

5a Write the words in numbers.

1	sixty thousand	_60,000_
2	five thousand six hundred	_____
3	three thousand	_____
4	three hundred and five	_____
5	nine point six	_____
6	two hundred and fifty-three thousand	_____
7	sixty-two million	_____
8	two hundred and forty-seven	_____
9	two billion	_____
10	nine hundred and sixty-three	_____

b Write the numbers in words.

1	53,000	_fifty-three thousand_
2	675	_____
3	3,000,000	_____
4	8.5	_____
5	348	_____
6	2,000,000,000	_____
7	5,600	_____
8	105	_____
9	350,000	_____
10	80,000,000	_____

6a 🎧 **11.2 Listen and circle the numbers you hear.**

1 40 / (50)
2 505 / 105
3 700 / 7,000
4 230 / 2,300
5 300,000 / 400,000
6 7,000,000 / 11,000,000

b 🎧 **11.3 Listen and write the numbers you hear.**

1 _____704_____
2 _____
3 _____
4 _____
5 _____
6 _____
7 _____
8 _____

Pronunciation
Big numbers

7a 🎧 **11.4 Listen to the words in the box. Practise saying them.**

nine   nineteen   a hundred   a thousand
a million   a billion

b 🎧 **11.5 Listen to the numbers. Practise saying them.**

1 sixty
2 six hundred
3 six hundred and five
4 six thousand
5 six point five

c 🎧 **11.6 Practise saying the numbers. Then listen and check.**

1 80
2 8,000
3 80,000
4 8,000,000
5 8,000,000,000

8 🎧 **11.7 Practise saying the numbers. Then listen and check.**

1 1.5
2 7.4
3 80
4 103
5 1,000
6 23,000
7 300,000
8 10,000,000

Grammar focus 1
Question words

9 Complete the questions with the question words in the box.

Where   How long   How   How much
What kind   How many   What   When
How old   Which

1 **A:** ____Where____ is Brisbane?
  B: It's in Australia.
2 **A:** _____ of tree is that?
  B: It's a palm tree.
3 **A:** _____ did you go to South America?
  B: Four years ago.
4 **A:** _____ coat is yours?
  B: The long black one.
5 **A:** _____ was the film?
  B: Two and a half hours.
6 **A:** _____ eggs do we need?
  B: About six.
7 **A:** _____ is your grandmother?
  B: She's 93.
8 **A:** _____'s your sister's name?
  B: Maria.
9 **A:** _____ do I switch this off?
  B: Press the red button.
10 **A:** _____ did your jacket cost?
  B: I can't remember. But it was expensive!

10 Put the words in the correct order to make questions.

1 are there / in / How / many / the USA / states ?
  How many states are there in the USA?
2 did / films / How many / make / he ?
  _____
3 a football match / does / How / last / long ?
  _____
4 the boxer / Mohammed Ali / born / was / Where ?
  _____
5 from / How far / here / your home / is ?
  _____
6 do / of / What kind / like / you / music ?
  _____
7 can / a / cheetah / fast / run /How ?
  _____
8 the world / is / in / the biggest / ocean / What ?
  _____

11 Complete the questions with the words in the box.

~~are~~   did (x2)   were   can   is   do   was

1 Where __are__ my glasses?
2 How _____ you get to school this morning?
3 How often _____ you go to the cinema?
4 How fast _____ the motorbike?
5 How many people _____ there at the party last night?
6 How many languages _____ you speak?
7 When _____ you start learning English?
8 Who _____ president in 1978?

Ships of the desert

Perhaps they aren't the most beautiful animals in the world, but in the hot lands of North Africa and the Middle East they are certainly one of the most useful. But how much do you know about camels? Camels normally live for about 40 years, but they usually stop working when they are about 25. Camels don't normally like running – it's too hot – but when they need to, they can run at 20 kilometres an hour. The dromedary, or Arabian camel, has got one hump. The Bactrian, or Asian camel, has longer hair and has got two humps. There are about 14 million camels in the world and most of them are dromedaries. An adult camel is about 2.1 metres tall and weighs about 500 kilograms. Camels can walk for more than 600 kilometres without drinking. They only need to drink water every six or eight days. But when there is water, they can drink up to 90 litres!

12 Read the text and write questions for the answers.

1 A: How _long do camels live_ ?
  B: For about 40 years.
2 A: When _____
    _____ ?
  B: When they are about 25.
3 A: How _____
    _____ ?
  B: About 20 kilometres an hour.
4 A: How _____
    _____ ?
  B: One.
5 A: How _____
    _____ ?
  B: 14 million.
6 A: How _____
    _____ ?
  B: 2.1 metres.
7 A: How _____
    _____ ?
  B: About 500 kilograms.
8 A: How _____
    _____ ?
  B: More than 600 kilometres.
9 A: How _____
    _____ ?
  B: Every six or eight days.
10 A: How _____
    _____ ?
  B: Up to 90 litres.

13 Complete the sentences with *How much*, *How many*, *Which* or *What*.

1 _What_ are you studying at university?
2 _____ aunts and uncles have you got?
3 There's chocolate or vanilla ice cream for dessert. _____ do you prefer?
4 _____ milk do you want in your coffee?
5 There's a bus at nine o'clock and another one at eleven o'clock. _____ is better for you?
6 _____ time did you spend in Africa?
7 _____ people were there at the meeting?
8 _____ does a kilo of cheese cost?
9 _____ is the capital of Vietnam?
10 _____ kind of camel has got two humps?
11 _____ languages do you speak?
12 _____ did the tickets cost?

Grammar focus 2

Quantifiers: *a lot of, a little, a few, not any, not much, not many*

14a Read the phone conversation between Pierre and his father and choose the correct answers.

D = Dad   **P** = Pierre

D: So, what did you do at the weekend, Pierre?
P: I had a party in my flat.
D: Really? How many people did you invite?
P: Well, I asked ¹*a few / any* friends.
D: What, about five? Ten?
P: No, I asked about 25 people.
D: Twenty-five! That's ²*a little / a lot of* people! And your flat's very small – you haven't got ³*many / much* space for 25 people.
P: There weren't 25 people.
D: Oh, that's good. So ⁴*a few / not many* people didn't come. Is that right?
P: No, everyone came. But some people brought ⁵*a few / a little* friends, too.
D: What?
P: So, there were about forty people.
D: What? Forty people in your very small flat? Oh no, poor you! That's terrible!
P: No, it was brilliant!
D: So, was it expensive? Did the party cost ⁶*not much / a lot of* money?
P: No, it didn't cost me ⁷*a few / any* money!
D: What? But 40 people eat ⁸*a lot of / not many* food!
P: No, they ate ⁹*a few / a little* bread and cheese, but that's all.
D: But weren't they hungry?
P: I don't know. I didn't have ¹⁰*much / a little* food in the fridge. So, they didn't eat much.
D: So, what did you all do?
P: We listened to ¹¹*a lot of / many* really good music. And we danced! It was brilliant!

b 🎧 **11.8** Listen and check.

15 Find and correct the mistakes in five of the sentences.

1 I didn't take many photographs. ☑

2 There isn't a much water in the river. ☐
   There isn't much water in the river.

3 There are a lot of big lakes in Canada. ☐

4 I only have a little of time at the weekend. ☐

5 Look! There was a lot of snow in the night. ☐

6 You can see a lot of animals in your garden. ☐

7 Maria's house has got a lot of the bedrooms. ☐

8 We don't watch not many programmes on TV. ☐

9 We went on an elephant safari, but we didn't see any elephants! ☐

10 There weren't many of people at the station this morning. ☐

16 Complete the sentences with *a lot of, much* or *any* and a word from the box.

~~animals~~   coffee   friends   time   food   girls

1 We didn't see many interesting plants on our wildlife holiday, but we saw ___*a lot of animals*___ .
2 I'm sorry, I'm very busy and can't meet you this week. I haven't got _____ .
3 Ismail is very sociable – he's got _____ .
4 I need to go shopping. I looked in the fridge, but it was empty. There wasn't _____ .
5 In John's class, there are only a few boys, but there are _____ .
6 She drinks a lot of tea, but she doesn't drink _____ .

Vocabulary
Celebrations and parties

1 Match descriptions 1–6 with the celebrations in the box.

> national holiday   birthday party
> wedding party   religious holiday
> graduation party   leaving party

1 All the schools were closed on Republic Day and hundreds of people dressed up in costumes and took part in a big parade through the town.
national holiday

2 Every year, people go to the temple. They buy pictures of Ganesh, the elephant god.
_____

3 Anji wore a beautiful white dress and Tom wore a suit. They were a lovely couple. The band played and all the guests danced.
_____

4 We had a little party to say goodbye to Alan after ten years in the office. Everyone said goodbye and wished him luck with the new job.
_____

5 We had lots of parties at university, but this last one was bigger and better. All the new graduates dressed up and their parents came, too.
_____

6 On the day I was ten, my school friends came to my house. My mother made me a cake and everyone sang _Happy Birthday_.
_____

Grammar focus 1
going to for future intentions

2a Look at the pictures and write sentences about the people. Use _going to_ and the phrases in the box.

> have a baby   have lunch   take a bus   go back inside
> read a newspaper   paint the ceiling   go to bed   play tennis

1 She _'s going to have a baby_ .

2 He _____ .

3 They _____ .

4 They _____ .

5 They _____ .

6 He _____ .

7 They _____ .

8 They _____ .

b 🎧 **12.1 Listen and check. Practise saying the sentences.**

3a Put the words in the correct order to make sentences.

1 going / to / She's / new / buy / a / bicycle
She's going to buy a new bicycle.

2 What / to / tomorrow / are / you / going / do ?
_____

3 isn't / have / to / a / going / She / party / leaving
_____

4 Are / you / to / shower / a / have / going ?
_____

5 We're / to / go / for / not / going / a / walk
_____

6 Bob / are / going / and / I / business / to / start / a
_____

7 to / come / going / to / aren't / They / the / party
_____

8 Why / you / going / aren't / house / to / move ?
_____

b 🎧 12.2 Listen and check.

4 Complete the sentences with *going to* and the word in brackets.

1 Mathias is 14 next month. He __*'s going to have*__ (have) a birthday party.

2 I've got a plane ticket. I _____ (fly) to Hawaii.

3 Good news: Chris and Jane are engaged! They _____ (get) married next August.

4 My dad's a teacher. But I _____ (not be) a teacher – I _____ (be) a businessman.

5 They went out for a meal at Fat Harry's Restaurant. But the food was expensive and not very good, so they _____ (not eat) there again.

6 We've got opera tickets for tonight. We _____ (see) *Rigoletto* by Verdi.

7 We _____ (not go) to Jake's party. It's a long journey and the party starts very late.

8 I _____ (stay) at home tonight.

Pronunciation
Weak forms of *to*

5 🎧 12.3 Listen to the pronunciation of *to* with the weak form /tə/. Practise saying the sentences.

1 We're going to go to France next year.
2 I'm going to study maths at university.
3 My sister's going to be a dentist.
4 What time are you going to come home tonight?
5 We're not going to have any parties this year.
6 She's going to go to the hairdresser's tomorrow.
7 What are you going to see at the cinema?
8 There's going to be a big parade.

Vocabulary
Weather and seasons

6 Read the sentences and describe the weather.

1 You're going to need your umbrellas if you go out.
It's raining./It's wet.

2 Can you pass me my sunglasses? That's better. Now I can see!
_____

3 Thirty-five degrees? Let's go for a swim!
_____

4 Please drive carefully. In some places you can't see more than five metres.
_____

5 What a beautiful spring day! Let's go for a walk.
_____

6 The weather's not too bad today; there's no sun, but it isn't raining.
_____

7 Look outside! The garden is completely white!
_____

8 Put on your warm clothes if you go out.
_____

9 All the leaves are falling off the trees!
_____

7a Add letters to complete the types of weather

1 h o t	6 s _ _ n y
2 f o g _ _	7 r _ _ n i n g
3 s n o _ _ n g	8 i _ y
4 c _ _ d	9 w i n d _
5 w _ t	10 c l _ _ d y

b Match words 1–10 in exercise a with pictures A–J.

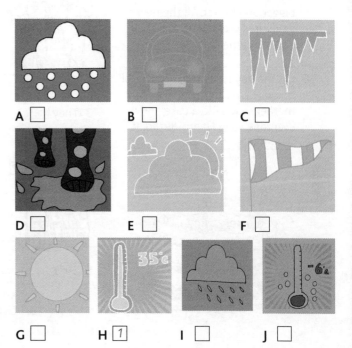

A ☐   B ☐   C ☐

D ☐   E ☐   F ☐

G ☐   H ☑1   I ☐   J ☐

Listen and read

8a 🎧 **12.4 Listen and read the world weather report.**

The world weather report

March 15th

There was heavy snow and windy weather in Chicago on Monday and there was also heavy rain on the west coast of the United States, particularly in and around the city of San Francisco.

Things were no better on the other side of the world, in Australia. There was extremely heavy rain in the state of Queensland, with 475 mm of rain falling in just five days.

In south-west Europe, there was more hot, sunny weather with the town of Jerez de la Frontera in the south of Spain the hottest place. The temperature was 30 degrees, the warmest so far this year.

It wasn't all good news in Europe, however. There was heavy snow in the Balkans and parts of north-eastern Italy on Monday and Tuesday. Things are getting a little better in the city of Irkutsk, in eastern Siberia, however: the temperature went above zero degrees for the first time since last November.

b Read the report again and complete the table.

	What was the weather like?	Extra information
Chicago	snow, windy	
San Francisco		
Queensland		475 mm of rain in five days
Jerez de la Frontera		
The Balkans		
North-east Italy		
Irkutsk		

Grammar focus 2
would like to and *want to* for future wishes

9 Complete the sentences with the correct form of *want to*.

1 _____Do you want to_____ (you) go to the cinema this evening? There's nothing good on TV.
2 I'm really not hungry. I _____ eat anything, thank you.
3 Valerie isn't going to look for a job when she leaves school. She _____ go to university.
4 _____ (anybody) go for a cup of coffee when the lesson finishes?
5 _____ (your friends) go for a walk before we have dinner?
6 Patricia is very tired. She _____ go home and go to bed.
7 He _____ be a waiter, but it's the only job he can find.
8 What _____ (you) do tonight?

10a Put the words in the correct order to make sentences with *would like to* and *want to*.

1 would like / a footballer / to be / when he's older / Stephen
   Stephen would like to be a footballer when he's older.
2 to / you / us / like / join / Would ?
   _____
3 We'd / book / like / to / please / a table,
   _____
4 want / doesn't / stay / at home / to / Marc
   _____
5 this evening / to see / like / film / Which / would you ?
   _____
6 a / taxi, / order / I'd / to / please / like
   _____
7 We / here / to / stay / want / don't
   _____
8 in the park / you / Would / like / for a walk / to go ?
   _____

b 🎧 12.5 Listen and check. Practise saying the sentences.

11 Correct the sentences. Add one extra word.

would
1 Françoise ʌ like to go to Japan one day.
2 Lisa's very shy. She doesn't to go to the party.
3 Where do you want go?
4 Would you to go out for lunch?
5 Chris isn't enjoying his holiday – he to go home.
6 What does he want do after university?
7 What would you like do tomorrow?
8 I like to find another job.

12a It is 9 a.m. on Wednesday. Put the future time expressions in the box in the correct order.

~~this afternoon~~   tonight   next month
tomorrow evening   next year   tomorrow morning
next week   this weekend

9 a.m. Wednesday
1 _____ *this afternoon* _____
2 _____
3 _____
4 _____
5 _____
6 _____
7 _____
8 _____

b It is now 4 p.m. on Friday 7th November 2014. What's another way to say:

1 10 a.m., Saturday 8th November?
   _____ *tomorrow morning* _____
2 9 p.m., Saturday 8th November?
   _____
3 The week 10–16th November?
   _____
4 Saturday and Sunday 8th and 9th November?
   _____
5 December 2014?
   _____
6 2015?
   _____
7 10 p.m., Friday 7th November?
   _____

Writing
Information to promote a festival

13 Look at the poster and write sentences about the festival. Use *going to* and some of the words and phrases in the box. Add your own ideas.

... are going to play ...   We've got a lot of ...
Visit our ...   There's/There are going to be ...
Find out more   take part in   competition
band   entertainer   parade

MUSIC FESTIVAL

2ND–4TH MARCH

The Town Park, Castle Road

Great local and international bands!

Competitions

Games for children

Tickets on sale from 15th January

Tel: 020 69585771

Language live
Suggestions and offers

14a Complete the sentences with the words in the box.

~~Shall~~	'll	about	don't
Let's	Why		

1 _Shall_ I cook something?
2 _____ go to a football match.
3 Why _____ we phone and book tickets?
4 How _____ going to the music festival this weekend?
5 I _____ ask Sarah to come.
6 _____ don't you make some coffee?

b **Match questions 1–6 in exercise a with answers a–f.**

a Yes, OK then. We all love sport.
b That sounds like a good idea. I'm hungry.
c OK. My favourite band is playing on Saturday.
d No! I made it last time! Why don't you make it?
e No, let's get the tickets online. We can save money.
f Good idea. Have you got her phone number?

c 🎧 **12.6 Listen and check.**

15a Complete the conversation with the words in the box.

~~shall~~	Let's	sounds	don't	about	we	Why	Shall

D = Dad   **A** = Anna   **N** = Nick   **M** = Mum

D: Well, everybody, what [1]_shall_ we do today? Any ideas?
A: I'm not sure – it depends on the weather. Is it sunny outside?
D: Just a minute ... No, not exactly. In fact, it's raining again!
N: [2]_____ don't we stay here? We can play computer games.
M: I know what we can do. [3]_____ have a look at the guidebook. I'm sure we can find some ideas in there.
D: That [4]_____ like a good idea. Well, there's the Museum of Country Life – how [5]_____ that?
N: Hmm ... is there anything more exciting?
D: Well, why [6]_____ we go to Aqua World?
N: Yes, that sounds better. [7]_____ we go there?
A: All right. It'll be fun.
M: Shall [8]_____ book tickets online? It's probably cheaper.
D: Good idea. So, everyone's happy!

b 🎧 **12.7 Listen and check.**

16 Write a similar conversation. Use the phrases in exercise 15 and your own ideas.

_____
_____
_____
_____
_____
_____
_____
_____
_____
_____
_____
_____
_____
_____
_____
_____
_____
_____
_____
_____

Vocabulary
School and university subjects

1 Match textbook extracts 1–16 with the subjects in the box.

design and technology   engineering   geography
languages   performing arts   business studies
science   medicine   law   history
information technology   leisure and tourism
literature   media studies   economics   maths

> It is easy to make a wooden table.

1 *design and technology*

> To understand how buildings and bridges stand up, we need to remember that the great engineers …

2 _____

> The Atlantic Ocean is between Europe and America.

3 _____

> **M**any people would like to open a business. So why do only a few people do it? There are three reasons …

4 _____

> Water is H_2O.

5 _____

> Doctors only give antibiotics and other medicine when it is necessary.

6 _____

> French, Danish, Dutch and English all have the same word for taxi, with the same spelling.

7 _____

> After about three minutes, the dancers move faster, the musicians play faster and the lights become brighter.

8 _____

> In 1492, Columbus sailed west and landed in America.

9 _____

> A computer's memory is in microchips. One kind is ROM (Read Only Memory), and this …

10 _____

> Lawyers often remember the case of *Smith versus Hankton* in 2012. The judge sent Hankton to prison because …

11 _____

> **I**n 2011, 29 million foreign visitors went on holiday to Britain. This was 30 percent more than in 2001. But these visitors stayed for a shorter time. This was because the …

12 _____

> In his play *Romeo and Juliet*, Shakespeare wrote some beautiful poetry.

13 _____

> If a country has oil or gas, this is, of course, good for the economy.

14 _____

> $875 \div 43 = 20.3488$

15 _____

> 20 years ago, people advertised in newspapers, in magazines and on TV. Today, we advertise online. But is online advertising really cheaper and better?

16 _____

Grammar focus 1
have to and *don't have to*

2   Complete the sentences about the airline staff with *have/has to* or *don't/doesn't have to*.

Bruce is a member of the cabin crew.
1   He ____*has to*____ look after passengers.
2   He _____ use a computer.
3   He _____ look smart.

George is a pilot.
4   He _____ fly the plane.
5   He _____ serve food.
6   He _____ wear a uniform.

Alizia and Meera work at the airline's call centre near London.
7   They _____ wear a uniform.
8   They _____ travel a lot.

3a   Use the prompts to make questions with *have to*. Then write short answers for the questions.

1   Bruce / look after the passengers?
A: *Does Bruce have to look after the passengers?*
B: *Yes, he does.*
2   he / use a computer?
A: _____
B: _____
3   he / look smart?
A: _____
B: _____
4   George / fly the plane?
A: _____
B: _____
5   he / serve food?
A: _____
B: _____
6   he / wear a uniform?
A: _____
B: _____
7   Alizia and Meera / wear a uniform?
A: _____
B: _____
8   they / travel a lot?
A: _____
B: _____

b   🎧 **13.1 Listen and check. Practise saying the questions and short answers.**

4a   Look at the table and complete the sentences about Denmark and Danish people. Use *have/has to* and *don't/doesn't have to*.

	In Denmark	In my country
1 Do men have to join the army?	✓	
2 Do women have to join the army?	✗	
3 Does a new driver have to take a driving test?	✓	
4 Do people have to go to school when they are 17?	✗	
5 Do schoolchildren have to study English?	✓	
6 Do you have to have a passport to leave the country?	✗	
7 Does there have to be an election every year?	✗	

1   Men ____*have to*____ join the army.
2   Women _____ join the army.
3   A new driver _____ take a driving test.
4   People _____ go to school when they are 17.
5   Schoolchildren _____ study English.
6   You _____ have a passport to leave the country.
7   There _____ be an election every year.

b   Complete the table in exercise a about your country. Then write sentences about your country using *have/has to* and *don't/doesn't have to*.

1   Men _____ .
2   Women _____ .
3   A new driver _____ .
4   People _____ .
5   Schoolchildren _____ .
6   You _____ .
7   There _____ .

Pronunciation
have to

5 🎧 **13.2 Listen to the pronunciation of** *have to* **in the sentences. Practise saying the sentences.**

1 Sorry, but I have to go now.
2 How long do you have to wait?
3 We have to get some petrol.
4 She doesn't have to make an appointment.
5 They have to get up at 5 o'clock tomorrow.
6 You have to see this film – it's brilliant!
7 I'm lucky – I don't have to work long hours.
8 You don't have to earn lots of money.

Vocabulary
Education and training

6 **Match 1–10 with a–j to make phrases.**

1 fail
2 get into
3 get
4 do
5 choose
6 apply
7 have an
8 train
9 be
10 earn

1	e
2	☐
3	☐
4	☐
5	☐
6	☐
7	☐
8	☐
9	☐
10	☐

a a course (in media studies)
b money
c university
d a career (in engineering)
e an exam
f for a job or course
g to be (a chef)
h interview
i a university degree
j unemployed

7 **Choose the correct answers.**

More and more people in the UK are getting ¹(**into**)/ **at** university. In the past, men often applied ²**for** / **to** courses in engineering or science and women trained to ³**do** / **be** nurses and teachers. But this has changed and women are now ⁴**ordering** / **choosing** different careers. More women are now doing courses ⁵**in** / **to** engineering, maths and information technology.
At university, women do better than men. More men than women fail their ⁶**universities** / **exams**. And more women ⁷**get** / **give** a degree (50 percent of women, but only 40 percent of men). So one thing is difficult to understand: why do men ⁸**earn** / **do** more money than women?

8 **Look at the careers website for young people. Complete the questions and answers with the words in the box.**

~~failed~~	do	degree	into	in	'm
interview	earn	a	applied		

○ ○ ○

Career advice

Q and A page

Q

I'm 18. I ¹ *failed* my exams at school. So now I can't get ²_____ university and I'm worried.
Aidan

A

Hi Aidan,
University is good for some people. But it's not for everyone. You can ³_____ lots of courses at colleges, so you don't have to go to university. The important thing is to choose ⁴_____ career first. Then you can decide.

Q

I left school in the summer and now I ⁵_____ unemployed. But I've got an ⁶_____ next week – it's for a job in a call centre. It's my first interview and I'm worried about it. What will they ask me?
Sharon

A

Sharon, lots of people don't like interviews. Don't worry! Just tell them why you ⁷_____ for the job and what you're good at. And good luck!

Q

Hi! But I don't know what to do: start a job in a bank or do a course ⁸_____ economics at university? I want to ⁹_____ lots of money in my career.
Thanks for any help,
Zak

A

Hello Zak,
It's usually good to get a ¹⁰_____ , so university might be right for you. But not everybody with a degree earns lots of money, so you have to work hard!

Listen and read

9a 🎧 **13.3** Read and listen to the text about the five ages of English.

The five ages of English

1   Old English

From about the 9th century, the Vikings, who lived in what is now Sweden, Norway and Denmark, began to arrive in the north of England. The language people spoke began to change. In the south of England, people began to translate books from Latin into English.

2   Middle English

In 1066, the Normans invaded England and French became the official language. Most educated people had to speak three languages: French, Latin and English. At this time, English literature began to develop. One of the most famous writers was the poet Geoffrey Chaucer, in the 14th century. His language is a little like the English of today.

3   Early Modern English (1450–1750)

This period includes the time of William Shakespeare, England's greatest writer. By the end of the 17th century, great scientists like Isaac Newton wrote in English, not in Latin. The British Empire began and the English language travelled across the Atlantic to North America and across Asia to India.

4   Modern English (1750–1950)

English was now a national language. The first dictionary, *Johnson's Dictionary*, appeared in 1755 and the first grammar books appeared soon after. As the British Empire grew in the 19th century, English became a more international language. People began to learn English around the world. The first English language textbooks appeared in the 1930s.

5   Late Modern English (from 1950)

Now, English language teaching is an important international industry. After World War II, the United States became the most important economic and cultural power in the world and a world market in audio-visual communication began. CNN International began in 1989 and the internet developed in the 1990s. English became a global language, with about two billion speakers.

b Read the text again and match pictures A–E with paragraphs 1–5.

A Isaac Newton

B newsreader on CNN

C Vikings talking to each other

D Dr Johnson's dictionary

E knight reading Chaucer

Grammar focus 2
might and *will*

10a Rewrite the sentences using *might* or *might not*.

1 Perhaps we'll go swimming this afternoon.
We *might go swimming this afternoon* .

2 It's possible that the plane will arrive late.
The plane _____ .

3 Maybe you'll be rich one day if you work hard.
You _____ .

4 It's possible that I won't be able to come to class next week.
I _____ .

5 I possibly won't see Frank this weekend.
I _____ .

6 Perhaps Philip won't stay until the end of the course.
Philip _____ .

7 The government will possibly change soon.
The government _____ .

8 Maybe the exam won't be as difficult as you think.
The exam _____ .

b 🎧 **13.4 Listen and check. Practise saying the sentences.**

11 Put the words in brackets in the correct order to complete the sentences.

1 I think ____*it will rain*____ (rain / it / will) – look at those dark clouds.

2 What _____ (do / will / you) after university?

3 Oh no! _____ (won't / We / be) on time.

4 What time _____ (will / finish / he) work tonight?

5 _____ (be / Will / there) any food at the party?

6 Sorry, but _____ (I / get / 'll) home late tonight.

7 _____ (Will / need / I) an umbrella?

8 She doesn't work very hard – _____ (won't / she / pass) her exams.

12 Put the words in the correct order to make sentences.

1 a / be / It / tomorrow / will / nice day
It will be a nice day tomorrow.

2 time / won't / There / to stop for lunch / be
_____

3 We'll / you / again / week / see / next
_____

4 need / your / You / umbrella / won't
_____

5 be / tomorrow / I / work / at / won't / Sorry, but
_____

6 soon / There / be / an election / will
_____

7 I / do / a / might / IT / course / in
_____

8 be / here / might / not / the / at / They / weekend
_____

13 Look at the information about three school friends who have just finished their exams. Write sentences with *might*, *might not*, *will probably* or *won't*.

Meg   Tom   Sampath

	Holiday?	University?	Job?
Meg	Spain with my parents	next year	all my family are doctors, but it's not for me!
Tom	no plans – Italy maybe?	maybe not!	for my father's company
Sampath	no time	not sure – perhaps get a job abroad instead?	who knows – an actor?

1 Meg *will probably go to Spain with her parents* .
(go to Spain)

2 Tom _____ .
(go to Italy)

3 Sampath
_____ .
(have time for a holiday)

4 Meg _____
(go to university)

5 Tom _____
(go to university)

6 Sampath _____
(get a job abroad instead)

7 Meg _____
(become a doctor)

8 Tom _____
(work for his father's company)

9 Sampath _____ .
(become an actor)

Vocabulary
Ways of communicating

1 Choose the correct answers.

1 She has to **make** / **do** a phone call.
2 I've updated my **landline** / **status** on my social networking site.
3 You made a mistake – you didn't send the **attachment** / **internet**.
4 I always keep my **smartphone** / **laptop** in my pocket.
5 We got our first internet **pick up** / **connection** in 1999.
6 Where can I buy **a tablet computer** / **an email**?
7 My brother and I use video **chat** / **talk** a lot.
8 I phoned her, but she didn't answer, so I left her **a voice message** / **an attachment**.

Grammar focus 1
Present perfect (unfinished time)

2a Complete the grid with the past participles of the verbs. What is the mystery phrase?

1 sleep	6 take	11 give
2 make	7 drive	12 keep
3 lose	8 write	13 tell
4 stand	9 say	14 become
5 speak	10 come	15 see

```
 1 S  L  E  P  T
    2
   3
    4
    5
    6
    7
 8
    9
      10
    11
 12
 13
    14
      15
```

b 🎧 14.1 Listen and check. Practise saying the verbs.

3 Complete the sentences with the Present Perfect form of the verb in brackets.

1 Martin ___has sent___ (send) hundreds of emails to his favourite singer, Kyla.
2 Mark and Yumiko _____ (see) all of Kurosawa's films.
3 Oh no! I _____ (leave) the tickets at home!
4 Terry Guy _____ (write) more than 20 books.
5 Wei Tzu _____ (lose) her keys six times this year!
6 I _____ (not read) any of Shakespeare's plays, but I'd like to.
7 I'm sorry, but I _____ (forget) your name.
8 We _____ (check) our computers, but we cannot find your name.

4 Look at the table. Complete the sentences about the Women's Soccer World Cup with the Present perfect form of the verb in brackets.

Women's Soccer World Cup					
Year	Venue	Winners	Goals	Losers	Goals
1991	China	USA	2	Norway	1
1995	Sweden	Norway	2	Germany	0
1999	USA	USA (won on penalties)	0	China	0
2003	USA	Germany	2	Sweden	1
2007	China	Germany	2	Brazil	0
2011	Germany	Japan (won on penalties)	2	USA	2

1 There ___have been___ (be) six World Cups up to now.
2 The USA _____ (win) the competition twice.
3 They _____ (not have) the competition in South America.
4 Germany _____ (play) in three World Cup Finals.
5 The World Cup _____ (be) in China twice.
6 There _____ (be) two World Cups in Europe.
7 Germany and the USA _____ (play) in three finals.
8 China, Brazil and Sweden _____ (not win) the World Cup.
9 Norway _____ (score) three goals in the World Cup Finals.
10 There _____ (be) two finals which finished in a penalty competition.

5a Read the text and complete the questions. Then write short answers.

Richard Marshall and his wife Elaine are retired. Recently, they moved to a new house in Hexham, a town near Newcastle in the north of England. Richard was born in Hexham, but Elaine is originally from Aberdeen, a town in the north of Scotland.

Gordon Marshall, Richard and Elaine's son, was born in Newcastle, but he now lives with his wife and daughter in Leeds, a town about 150 km away, where he is a teacher. He's also worked abroad – he worked in a restaurant in France when he was younger.

Sarah Marshall, Gordon's wife, has always wanted her own business. Her daughter Rebecca left school last year and now they're in business together. She and her mother have opened a new sandwich shop called Crusts in Leeds city centre. It's the first time they've worked together!

1 A: _Has_ Richard always lived in Hexham?
   B: _Yes, he has._

2 A: _____ Elaine ever lived in another town?
   B: _____

3 A: _____ they always lived in the same house?
   B: _____

4 A: _____ Gordon always been a teacher?
   B: _____

5 A: _____ he ever worked abroad?
   B: _____

6 A: _____ Gordon and Sarah always lived in Leeds?
   B: _____

7 A: _____ Sarah had her own business before?
   B: _____

8 A: _____ Rebecca left school?
   B: _____

b 🎧 14.2 Listen and check. Practise saying the questions and short answers.

Vocabulary
Technology

6 Add letters to complete the technology words.

1 u _ l _ _ d
2 in _ _ _ n _ t a _ _ _ ss
3 user
4 W _ - _ i h _ _ sp _ t
5 a _ _ _ -vi _ _ _ s _ _ _ w _ re
6 d _ _ nl _ _ _ ed
7 p _ _ _ w _ _ d
8 h _ _ _ k _ r
9 v _ _ _ s

7 Complete the sentences with technology words from exercise 6.

1 I took some photos at the party yesterday – I'm going to _____ *upload* _____ them to my website now.

2 Does the hotel have a _____ ? I have to check my email.

3 A _____ had my username and password and he accessed my bank account.

4 I lost all my files because my computer had a _____ .

5 I need to buy some _____ . Then my computer will be safe.

6 I'm a typical _____ . I send emails, use video chat and surf the web, like most people.

7 Yesterday we _____ some great songs from the internet.

8 If you forget your _____ , we can email it to you; just give us your email address or username.

9 Sometimes I can't _____ the internet at home. I have to shut down my computer and then start it again.

Listen and read

8 🎧 14.3 Read and listen to the text about how three people keep in touch with friends and family.

Keeping in touch

Scott ||||||||||||||||||||||||||||||||||||||||||||||

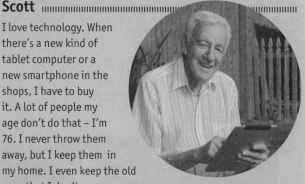

I love technology. When there's a new kind of tablet computer or a new smartphone in the shops, I have to buy it. A lot of people my age don't do that – I'm 76. I never throw them away, but I keep them in my home. I even keep the old ones that I don't use.

I only use one mobile, one tablet and one desktop computer. I use them a lot – I download films and music and I use social networking sites a lot. It's a good way to keep in touch with old friends. And it's helped me to make a lot of new friends, too.

Gerry ||||||||||||||||||||||||||||||||||||||||||

I live in Toronto, but my son and his kids live in New Zealand. I go there or they come to visit me every year. But we speak most days – video chat helps us to stay in touch. I think the kids – my grandchildren – like speaking to me on the screen. They're always very chatty and sociable.
But when we meet in Toronto or in New Zealand, they're shy. When I was young, my friends and I met and talked. Now young people go online. The world's changing!

Delvin ||||||||||||||||||||||||||||||||||||||||||

I love people and I hate computers. My only phone is a landline. Landline phones were OK for my parents and my grandparents, and they're OK for me!
I like to meet my friends, neighbours and family. When I want to talk to someone, I go to their home. If they're in, we have a chat. If they're not there, I come back home. I don't mind – I like walking! My sons and my grandchildren are always saying, 'Come on, you have to get a computer, you have to get a mobile – then you can do video chat!' Well, I don't want to use mobiles and computers and smartphones and the internet! I'm happy as I am.

9 Read the text again and answer the questions.

1 Who uses the internet to contact his family?
   Gerry

2 Who has a lot of electronic devices in his home?
   _____

3 Who thinks that technology is changing how people communicate?
   _____

4 Who doesn't have a mobile?
   _____

5 Who has more friends now because of the internet?
   _____

6 Who prefers to meet people than communicate with technology?
   _____

Grammar focus 2
Present perfect (with *ever*)

10a Complete the questions with the Present perfect form of the verbs in the box.

....

~~do~~   visit   be   have   buy   meet

....

1 Mum, have I ever _done_ anything really bad?
2 Have you ever _____ a painting from an artist?
3 Has there ever _____ a female Prime Minister in the United Kingdom?
4 Have you ever _____ a famous person?
5 Has your computer ever _____ a virus?
6 Have you ever _____ Ireland?

b Match questions 1–6 in exercise a with answers a–f.

a No, I haven't. I'm not really very interested in art. [2]
b Yes, you have! When you were about two years old, you were very naughty! ☐
c No, it hasn't. I've got anti-virus software on it. ☐
d Yes, there has. Margaret Thatcher in the 1980s. ☐
e Yes, I have. I went to Dublin last year and I had a great time. ☐
f No, I haven't. I saw Robbie Williams in concert, but I didn't speak to him! ☐

c 🎧 14.4 Listen and check.

11a Find and correct two mistakes in each conversation.

1 A: Have you ever be in love?
  B: Yes, I've. It was when I was 16.
   A: Have you ever been in love?
   B: Yes, I have. It was when I was 16.

2 A: Have you ever lose your wallet?
  B: No, I've never lost my wallet, but I has found some money on the street.

_____
_____
_____

3 A: Has your mum and dad ever travelled by plane?
  B: Yes, they were. They've flown to the USA twice.

_____
_____
_____

4 A: Has ever it snowed in Saudi Arabia?
  B: No, hasn't.

_____
_____
_____

b 🎧 **14.5** Listen and check.

12 Complete the questions with the Present perfect form of the verb in brackets. Then write short answers.

1 Roger Federer

1 A: ___*Has he ever won*___ (ever / win) an Olympic medal?
  B: Yes, _____*he has*_____ .

2 A: _____ (ever / act) in a film?
  B: No, _____ .

2 Brad Pitt and Angelina Jolie

3 A: _____ (ever / visit) Namibia?
  B: Yes, _____ .

4 A: _____ (ever / live) in Russia?
  B: No, _____ .

3 Rinat Shaham

5 A: _____ (ever / sing) at the Royal Opera House in Covent Garden, London?
  B: Yes, _____ .

6 A: _____ (ever / made) an album of rap music?
  B: No, _____ .

4 David Beckham

7 A: _____ (ever / be) in an advert?
  B: Yes, _____ .

8 A: _____ (ever / play) in a World Cup final?
  B: No, _____ .

Pronunciation
Strong and weak forms of *have*

13 🎧 **14.6 Read and listen to the conversation. Are the words in bold strong (/æ/) or weak (/ə/)?**

A: ¹**Have** you ever been on TV, Tom?

B: ²**Have** I been on TV? What a question! No, of course I ³**haven't**. Why? ⁴**Have** you ever been on TV?

A: Yes, I ⁵**have**.

B: No, you ⁶**haven't**!

A: Yes, I ⁷**have**!

B: Well, which TV show ⁸**have** you been on?

A: It wasn't a TV show. It was a football match last year – Scotland against Ukraine. I was in the crowd. And the match was on TV!

B: You and fifty thousand people! Sorry, no – you can't say you've been on TV.

A: I can!

1 _weak_
2 _____
3 _____
4 _____
5 _____
6 _____
7 _____
8 _____

Language live
Telephoning

14a Choose the correct answers.

A **A:** Hello?

B: Hello, ¹(*this is*)/ *that's* Francis here.

A: Oh hi, Francis. It's not a good moment to talk. ²*Am* / *Can* I call you back?

B: Yes, that's fine. Talk ³*soon* / *in the future*.

B **A:** Hello?

B: Good morning. Is ⁴*that* / *here* City Taxis? I'm calling ⁵*about* / *of* a taxi.

A: A taxi? But this is Dario's Pizza Bar. You've got the ⁶*bad* / *wrong* number.

B: Oh, I'm sorry. Bye.

A: That's OK. Bye.

C **A:** Hello? Mary ⁷*speaking* / *chatting*.

B: Hi, Mary. How are you?

A: I'm fine. Sorry, ⁸*who's* / *what's* that?

B: This is Diana here.

A: Oh yes, Diana! How are you?

B: I'm fine, thanks.

b 🎧 **14.7 Listen and check.**

Writing
A text message

15 Read the text messages from your friends Sam and Francis. Write replies to them using some of the 'text speak' in the box.

n	2	c u	u	wd	@	abt	4	gr8
luv	btw	r	ur	xx	tnx	2moro		

Hi! r u free to meet 2moro 4 coffee? Where? When? c u! Luv Sam xx

_____
_____
_____
_____
_____
_____

Hello. We're having a party this Saturday @ my home. Can u come? R u going 2 bring anyone? Let me know. Tnx! Francis

_____
_____
_____
_____
_____
_____

Audio script

UNIT 1 RECORDING 1

My name is John. I am married. My wife is from Vietnam and I am from Australia. Our children are six and eight years old. They are Australian and Vietnamese!

My wife and I are teachers. I am an English teacher and my wife is a French teacher. Our jobs are great – and the children in the school are very nice.

UNIT 1 RECORDING 3

Polish, Australian, American, Japanese, Chinese, British, Russian, Spanish, Irish, Brazilian, Vietnamese,

0UNIT 1 RECORDING 6

1 She's a police officer. She works in the police station.
2 He plays for Manchester United – he's a footballer.
3 Javier Bardem is an actor from Spain – he's in the film *Skyfall*.
4 Adele is a singer. Her album 21 is great.
5 Lang Lang is a musician from China. He plays the piano.
6 My cousin is a shop assistant in a supermarket.
7 My brother is a waiter in Franco's Pizza Restaurant.
8 He works in the hospital. He's a doctor.
9 My mum's a businesswoman and my dad's a businessman. They're in Tokyo this week, on business.

UNIT 1 RECORDING 7

1 What's your name?
2 Where are you from?
3 Are you here on business?
4 How old are you?
5 What's your telephone number?
6 Are you married?
7 What's your email address?
8 What's your job?

UNIT 1 RECORDING 8

I: Interviewer   AB: Au Van Bien
1 I: What's your full name?
   AB: My full name's Au Van Bien.
2 I: What's your job?
   AB: I'm an engineer.
3 I: What's your email address?
   AB: It's avb@tlctmail.org.
4 I: Where are you from?
   AB: I'm from Vietnam.
5 I: How old are you?
   AB: I'm 32.

UNIT 2 RECORDING 1

What have I got? Well, I've got a bag. And some coins – about five or six euros. And a credit card. They're in my wallet. And my glasses, of course. But not a dictionary. My dictionary's at home, not with me.

Err . . . well, I haven't got a watch. The time's on my phone and my mobile's always with me. And a memory stick – eight gigabytes, I think. Oh, and something to drink: a bottle of water. And – oh, excuse me, I'm sorry, some tissues. And also . . . I think . . . my . . . oh, my keys. My car keys and my keys to my flat. Oh . . . I haven't got my keys! Oh where are they?

UNIT 2 RECORDING 4

1 Look at that car.
2 Are these your glasses?
3 How much are those tissues?
4 This is my new phone. It's great!
5 Who's that man?
6 I'm Jonny and this is my email address.
7 Who are those people over there?
8 Look. These are my holiday photos.

UNIT 2 RECORDING 5

1 Silvia's got a dog. His name's Rex.
2 She's got a car. It's an Audi.
3 She hasn't got a computer.
4 Martin and Inge haven't got a pet.
5 They've got two cars.
6 They've got a computer.

UNIT 2 RECORDING 6

1 A: Has Silvia got a dog?
   B: Yes, she has.
2 A: Has she got a car?
   B: Yes, she has.
3 A: Has she got a computer?
   B: No, she hasn't.
4 A: Have Martin and Inge got a pet?
   B: No, they haven't.
5 A: Have they got a car?
   B: Yes, they have.
6 A: Have they got a computer?
   B: Yes, they have.

UNIT 2 RECORDING 9

1 What's your name?
2 Can you say that again, please?
3 How do you spell that?
4 What's your address?
5 What's your postcode?
6 Have you got a contact phone number?
7 How old are you?

UNIT 3 RECORDING 1

1   I get up early.
2   You live nearby.
3   They have a new phone number.
4   We work very hard.
5   I have a memory stick.
6   We live in a block of flats.
7   They study French at university.
8   We go to school by bus.
9   They have lunch in a café.
10 You go out in the evening.

UNIT 3 RECORDING 3

1 I don't work in an office. I work at home.
2 Bob and Jackie don't live in a city. They live in a small town.
3 We don't study economics. We study computer science.
4 My friends and I don't go to university by car. We go by bus.
5 I don't go out on weekdays. I go out at the weekend.
6 You don't have a small flat! You have a beautiful big flat!
7 I don't have a shower in the morning. I have a bath in the evening.
8 My cousins don't work in an office. They work in a shopping centre.

UNIT 3 RECORDING 4

1 A: Do you live in a big city?
   B: Yes, I do. There are nine million people in Bangkok.
2 A: Do you and your friends like Chinese food?
   B: Yes, we do. We go to Chinese restaurants every weekend.
3 A: Do you study economics?
   B: No, I don't. I'm not a student.
4 A: Do I work hard?
   B: Yes, you do. You're a very good student!
5 A: Do we live in a nice town?
   B: Yes, we do. I think it's beautiful.
6 A: Have you got an email address?
   B: Yes, I have. It's jhf@biggmail.com.

7 A: Do you get up early in the morning?
   B: No, I don't. I work in the evening and I get up late.
8 A: Do your cousins speak English?
   B: Yes, they do. They speak English and Italian.

UNIT 4 RECORDING 1

1 She comes from Japan.
2 She works as a fashion designer.
3 She lives in San Francisco.
4 She speaks Japanese and English.
5 She likes cooking and dancing.

UNIT 4 RECORDING 2

1 Maria doesn't like studying grammar.
2 It doesn't rain in summer.
3 My brother doesn't like getting up at seven o'clock.
4 The restaurant doesn't close on Sunday evening.
5 Martin doesn't come to class every week.
6 Tony doesn't buy all his food at the supermarket.
7 Carla doesn't drive to work.
8 My cousin doesn't visit me every month.

UNIT 4 RECORDING 4

1 A: Does your sister cycle?
   B: No, she doesn't. She doesn't have a bike.
2 A: Does she play sports?
   B: Yes, she does. She plays tennis and basketball.
3 A: Does your boyfriend like cooking?
   B: Yes, he does. He's a very good cook.
4 A: Does he often cook for you?
   B: No, he doesn't. I usually cook for him!
5 A: Has your father got a big car?
   B: Yes, he has. It's very big.
6 A: Does it go fast?
   B: No, it doesn't. It's old and slow.

UNIT 4 RECORDING 5

1 A: Where does he live?
   B: He lives in Oslo.
2 A: What does he do?
   B: He's an engineer.
3 A: Where does he work?
   B: He works in the city centre.
4 A: How does he go to work?
   B: He goes to work by bike.
5 A: What does Olaf's wife do?
   B: She's a doctor.
6 A: How does he spend his weekends?
   B: He spends his weekends with his family.

UNIT 4 RECORDING 7

1 A: Hi, Bea. This is Clara. She's my friend from university.
   B: Hello, Clara. I'm Bea. Nice to meet you.
   C: Nice to meet you, too.
2 A: Happy birthday! I know you like flowers, so these are for you.
   B: Oh, what nice flowers! Thank you so much! They're lovely!
3 A: Would you like something to drink?
   B: Yes, please. An orange juice, please.
   A: And a drink for you, Henri?
   C: No thanks, I'm fine.

UNIT 5 RECORDING 2

1 Thank you, sir. Here's your boarding pass. You have seat 17C.
2 Show your passport again when you go through security.
3 Please wait in Departures. Your flight is in one hour.
4 Look at the screen. There's our flight: KLM267 to Amsterdam, from gate 14. Let's go!

5 The plane is now ready. People with small children, please board the plane now.
6 Good morning, everyone, this is your pilot. Welcome on our flight to Amsterdam.
7 Hello again, everyone. This is your pilot. We are now at our destination. Welcome to Amsterdam!
8 Excuse me, I can't find my luggage – one suitcase and a blue bag.

UNIT 5 RECORDING 3

1 A: It's 8:30 in the morning. Can I park here?
   B: Yes, you can.
2 A: Can I park here on a Sunday?
   B: Yes, you can.
3 A: Can I smoke here?
   B: No, you can't.
4 A: Tom and Barbara are sixteen years old. Can they go in?
   B: No, they can't.
5 A: I'm nineteen years old. Can I go in?
   B: Yes, you can.
6 A: Can I cross the road now?
   B: Yes, you can.
7 A: I've got a dog. Can it come in?
   B: No, it can't.
8 A: Excuse me, can we buy a phonecard here?
   B: Yes, you can.

UNIT 5 RECORDING 4

1 Caroline can speak French.
2 She can't play chess.
3 She can't drive a car.
4 She can play a musical instrument.
5 Fabrizio can speak French.
6 He can play chess.
7 He can't drive a car.
8 He can't play a musical instrument.

UNIT 5 RECORDING 5

1 A: Can Kristina speak French?
   B: No, she can't.
2 A: Can she play chess?
   B: No, she can't.
3 A: Can she drive a car?
   B: Yes, she can.
4 A: Can she play a musical instrument?
   B: Yes, she can.
5 A: Can Max speak French?
   B: No, he can't.
6 A: Can he play chess?
   B: Yes, he can.
7 A: Can he drive a car?
   B: Yes, he can.
8 A: Can he play a musical instrument?
   B: No, he can't.

UNIT 5 RECORDING 7

1 A: What is the capital of Colombia?
   B: It's Bogotá.
2 A: In India, do people drive on the left or on the right?
   B: They drive on the left.
3 A: Which languages do they speak in Canada?
   B: They speak English and French.
4 A: How many grams are there in a kilogram?
   B: One thousand.
5 A: Where is Haneda Airport?
   B: It's in Tokyo, Japan.
6 A: Who is Daniel Craig?
   B: He's a British actor. He plays James Bond in *Skyfall* and other films.

Audio script

7 A: How far is it from the Earth to the Moon?
   B: It's 380,000 kilometres.
8 A: How long does it take to boil an egg?
   B: It takes about five minutes.
9 A: What are the four countries in the UK?
   B: England, Scotland, Wales and Northern Ireland.
10 A: What's the name of the big river in Budapest?
   B: In English, it's the Danube.

UNIT 6 RECORDING 1

1 A: Is there a swimming pool?
   B: Yes, there is.
2 A: Are there any places to eat and drink?
   B: Yes, there are.
3 A: Is there a beach?
   B: No, there isn't.
4 A: Is there a children's playground?
   B: Yes, there is.
5 A: Are there any supermarkets?
   B: No, there aren't.

UNIT 6 RECORDING 3

1 There's a good Chinese restaurant near my house.
2 There are some tomatoes on the table.
3 There's a bus stop near here.
4 There's some cheese in the fridge.
5 There are some good vegetarian cafés in my city.
6 Yes, there are.
7 There's a food programme on TV tonight.
8 There's a phone call for you.

UNIT 6 RECORDING 5

1 fish and chips
2 fruit and vegetables
3 herbs and spices
4 sweet and sour
5 knife and fork
6 tea and coffee
7 food and drink
8 salt and pepper
9 bread and butter

UNIT 6 RECORDING 6

1 A: My son is three. He eats with a plastic knife and fork.
   B: Really? My daughter just eats with her hands!
2 A: I want a sandwich. We've got some cheese, but is there any bread and butter?
   B: No, there isn't. Have an apple!
3 A: Hi, it's me. I'm in the supermarket. Do we need any fruit and vegetables?
   B: Yes, we do. Grapes and carrots, please.
4 A: I love cooking with herbs and spices. Garlic, pepper and turmeric are my favourites.
   B: Really? Well, you can cook dinner tonight, then!
5 A: When you go to the mountains, take lots of food and drink with you. There aren't any shops in the mountains.
   B: Yes, Mum!
6 A: What would you like to drink with your breakfast, sir? We've got fruit juice and tea and coffee, of course.
   B: A black coffee, please.

UNIT 6 RECORDING 7

1 A: How much sugar is there?
   B: There isn't much – I think we need some more.
2 A: How much meat do you eat?
   B: I have chicken, lamb or beef every day.

3 A: How many potatoes and carrots are there?
   B: There are a lot of potatoes, but there aren't any carrots.
4 A: How much fat is there in cheese?
   B: Most cheese is about 40 percent fat.
5 A: How much salt can we eat?
   B: Only about six grams a day.
6 A: How many eggs do I need?
   B: Three.
7 A: How much coffee would you like?
   B: One small cup, please.
8 A: How many Indian restaurants are there in the UK?
   B: About 10,000. There are 1,000 in London.

UNIT 6 RECORDING 8

1 A: How many stars are there on the Australian flag?
   B: There are six stars on the Australian flag.
2 A: How much skin does the average person have?
   B: One and a half to two square metres.
3 A: How much food does an adult elephant eat each day?
   B: 135 kilos.
4 A: How many people use Atlanta Airport, USA, every day?
   B: 252,000.
5 A: How many brothers has Prince William got?
   B: He's got one: Prince Harry.
6 A: How much water is there in the Sea of Crisis?
   B: There isn't any – the Sea of Crisis is on the moon.
7 A: How many people live in Japan?
   B: The population of Japan is about 127 million.
8 A: How many cars are there in the world?
   B: There are over one billion.
9 A: How much cheese does the average French person eat each year?
   B: About 24 kilos of cheese.
10 A: How many stations are there on the Moscow Metro?
   B: There are 186 stations.

UNIT 6 RECORDING 9

1 A: Can I have one of those, please?
   B: One of these chocolate cakes? Yes, here you are.
2 A: I'd like one cheese sandwich, please.
   B: Eat-in or takeaway?
   A: Eat-in, please.
3 A: Hello, I'd like a coffee, please.
   B: Sure. Cappuccino, filter coffee or espresso?
   A: Espresso, please.
4 A: Can I have one banana muffin, please?
   B: OK. That's £1.85, please.
5 A: Can we have two pizzas, please?
   B: OK. Would you like anything else?
   A: No, thanks.
6 A: Right, that's nine euros twenty cents.
   B: Nine euros twenty? Here's ten euros. Keep the change.
   A: Oh, thanks very much!

UNIT 7 RECORDING 1

1 In 2012, the Olympic Games were in London. True.
2 The Berlin Wall was in Russia. False. The Berlin Wall wasn't in Russia. It was in Germany.
3 The winner of the 2012 US election was Mitt Romney. False. The winner wasn't Mitt Romney. The winner was Barack Obama.
4 The Beatles were famous in the 1940s. False. The Beatles weren't famous in the 1940s. They were famous in the 1960s.
5 The world football champions in 2010 were Spain. True.
6 Steve Jobs was the boss of Microsoft. False. Steve Jobs wasn't the boss of Microsoft. He was the boss of Apple.
7 Nelson Mandela was the president of South Africa. True.
8 Daniel Radcliffe was in the James Bond films. False. Daniel Radcliffe wasn't in the James Bond films. He was in the Harry Potter films.

UNIT 7 RECORDING 2

1 A: Was Mark Twain a painter?
   B: No, he wasn't.
2 A: Was he American?
   B: Yes, he was.
3 A: Was Charlie Chaplin born in the USA?
   B: No, he wasn't.
4 A: Was he an actor?
   B: Yes, he was.
5 A: Were the Marx Brothers born in the USA?
   B: No, they weren't.
6 A: Were they comedians?
   B: Yes, they were.
7 A: Was Anna Pavlova Russian?
   B: Yes, she was.
8 A: Was she a singer?
   B: No, she wasn't.
9 A: Were Pelé and Jairzinho from Argentina?
   B: No, they weren't.
10 A: Were they footballers?
   B: Yes, they were.

UNIT 7 RECORDING 3

A: Hi. Where were you yesterday?
B: I was in the library.
A: What? No, you weren't in the library!
B: Yes, I was.
A: Well, I didn't see you. I was there all day from eight to five.
B: No, that's not true. The library doesn't open at eight o'clock. It opens at nine o'clock every day.
A: Oh yes, you're right. I was there from nine to five.
B: Really? Well, I was there at one o'clock. And you weren't there!
A: Oh yes, that's right, too. I wasn't in the library then. I was in town.
B: Who were you in town with?
A: I was with Roberto. We went for lunch. Then I was in the library again from two to five.
B: Oh right. I wasn't there for long. I went home at about half past one.
A: So, where are you now?
B: In the library. Where are you?
A: In bed!

UNIT 7 RECORDING 5

Seventy years ago, Amelia Earhart was America's favourite woman. In 1932, she flew across the Atlantic Ocean alone: the first woman to do this.

Her journey started in Newfoundland, Canada: fifteen hours later, her Lockheed Vega aeroplane arrived in Londonderry, Northern Ireland. People all over the world wanted to meet this incredible woman. She met King George V of England and became friends with the US President, Franklin D. Roosevelt. The American people loved her.

Five years later, Amelia tried to fly around the world. An American University gave her $50,000 for a new Lockheed Electra aeroplane. On the morning of July 2nd 1937, Amelia and her co-pilot, Fred Noonan left Lae, in New Guinea, and began their journey to Howland Island in the Pacific Ocean.

On July 3rd 1937, the American ship Itasca received a radio message from Amelia: a few minutes later her plane disappeared. American ships spent nearly two weeks looking for the plane, but they found nothing.

UNIT 8 RECORDING 1

1 A: Did Shakespeare write *Romeo and Juliet*?
   B: Yes, he did.
2 A: Did Alexander Graham Bell invent email?
   B: No, he didn't.
3 A: Did Marilyn Monroe sing *Candle in the Wind*?
   B: No, she didn't.
4 A: Did Captain Cook discover America?
   B: No, he didn't.

5 A: Did Leonardo da Vinci paint the Mona Lisa?
   B: Yes, he did.
6 A: Did Madonna play Evita?
   B: Yes, she did.
7 A: Did Beethoven write rock songs?
   B: No, he didn't.
8 A: Did Laurel and Hardy make comedy films?
   B: Yes, they did.
9 A: Did Yuri Gagarin travel to the moon?
   B: No, he didn't.

UNIT 8 RECORDING 2

1 A: Where did he go?
   B: He went to Paris.
2 A: How did he travel?
   B: By train.
3 A: Where did he have lunch?
   B: At The Station Buffet Restaurant.
4 A: How much did it cost?
   B: £15.95.
5 A: What did he buy at the station?
   B: Some books.
6 A: How many books did he buy?
   B: Two.
7 A: When did the train leave?
   B: At 2:30 p.m.
8 A: How long did the journey take?
   B: Two hours and sixteen minutes.

UNIT 8 RECORDING 5

Hi, everyone! It's my birthday on Thursday next week, so let's have an evening out to celebrate. I want to go to Pasta Express, so let's meet there. The meeting time is 7:30. See you there! Helen

UNIT 9 RECORDING 1

1 Brazil is bigger than Australia.
2 The River Mississippi is longer than the River Volga.
3 Blue whales are heavier than elephants.
4 The Pyramids in Egypt are older than the Parthenon in Greece.
5 The Burj Khalifa in Dubai is taller than the Eiffel Tower in Paris.
6 The Akashi-Kaikyo Bridge in Japan is longer than the Sydney Harbour Bridge in Australia.
7 Gold is more expensive than silver.
8 Esperanto is easier than English.

UNIT 9 RECORDING 3

A woman went into the most expensive butcher's in town and asked for the biggest chicken in the shop. The shopkeeper showed her a chicken and said 'This is the best chicken in the shop, madam.'

'It's very small,' she said. 'Have you got a larger one?'

'Just a moment,' said the shopkeeper. He took the chicken into another room. In fact it was the only chicken he had. So he put some sausages inside to make it look bigger.

'Here you are,' he said. 'This is our most delicious chicken. And you can see that it's bigger than the other. But I'm afraid it's also more expensive.'

'Hmm . . . but I'm not sure if it's better than the other. OK. Can I have both of them, please?'

UNIT 9 RECORDING 4

1 You can buy steak at a butcher's.
2 You can buy shirts, trousers and skirts at a clothes shop.
3 You can buy bread at a baker's.
4 You can buy stamps and send parcels at a post office.
5 You can buy medicine at a pharmacy.
6 You can have a haircut at a hairdresser's.
7 You can buy a present at a gift shop.
8 You can take your clothes for cleaning at a dry-cleaner's.

Audio script

UNIT 10 RECORDING 2

What am I wearing today? Oh well, I've got a brown skirt and a white shirt. It's cold, so I'm wearing a jumper to keep warm and a jacket. And it's very sunny today, so I'm wearing sunglasses, too. And I've got my baseball cap, so I'm ready to go out!

UNIT 10 RECORDING 3

1 The robot is cleaning the living room.
2 Veronica is looking out of the window.
3 She is talking to someone on her mobile phone.
4 The baby is sitting on the floor.
5 The baby is eating the flowers.
6 Ronald is having a cup of tea.
7 He is watching television.
8 The two older children are doing their homework.

UNIT 10 RECORDING 4

1 **A:** What are you doing?
  B: My homework.
2 **A:** Where are you going?
  B: To my English class.
3 **A:** Why are you smiling?
  B: Because you look so funny!
4 **A:** Who are you talking to?
  B: My brother.
5 **A:** What are you reading?
  B: Oh, nothing, just a magazine.
6 **A:** What are you watching?
  B: Sh! It's my favourite programme.

UNIT 10 RECORDING 5

S: Sophie   **J:** Jenny
S: It's me, Sophie.
J: Hi, Sophie. Where are you? What are you doing?
S: I'm at my sister's wedding.
J: Fantastic! Are you enjoying yourself?
S: No, I'm not! I'm not having a good time. It's awful!
J: Why? What's happening?
S: Well, there's the music for a start. They're playing this awful 80s music . . . and . . . oh no, I don't believe it. My dad's dancing with my mum's sister!
J: How about your mum? Is she dancing, too?
S: No, she isn't. She isn't doing anything. She's looking at my dad.
J: Oh dear!
S: Just a minute . . . there's a very good-looking young man over there. There's a girl talking to him but he isn't listening and . . . oh!
J: Sophie. What's he doing?
S: He's coming over! Talk to you later! 'Bye!!

UNIT 10 RECORDING 9

1 **A:** I'd like a haircut, please.
  B: OK. Do you have an appointment?
  A: Yes, I do.
2 **A:** How would you like your hair cut?
  B: Not too long and not too short, please.
3 **A:** How much do I owe you?
  B: That's a hundred euros, please. How would you like to pay?
  A: By credit card, please.
4 **A:** I tried this on, but it's too small. Have you got this in a larger size?
  B: Yes, here you are.
5 **A:** Look at this! What do you think?
  B: It's great. It suits you.
6 **A:** I'll take this one, please.
  B: OK. How would you like to pay?
  A: By credit card, please.

UNIT 12 RECORDING 1

1 She's going to have a baby.
2 He's going to read a newspaper.
3 They're going to play tennis.
4 They're going to take a bus.
5 They're going to go back inside.
6 He's going to go to bed.
7 They're going to paint the ceiling.
8 They're going to have lunch.

UNIT 12 RECORDING 2

1 She's going to buy a new bicycle.
2 What are you going to do tomorrow?
3 She isn't going to have a leaving party.
4 Are you going to have a shower?
5 We're not going to go for a walk.
6 Bob and I are going to start a business.
7 They aren't going to come to the party.
8 Why aren't you going to move house?

UNIT 12 RECORDING 5

1 Stephen would like to be a footballer when he's older.
2 Would you like to join us?
3 We'd like to book a table, please.
4 Marc doesn't want to stay at home.
5 Which film would you like to see this evening?
6 I'd like to order a taxi, please.
7 We don't want to stay here.
8 Would you like to go for a walk in the park?

UNIT 12 RECORDING 6

1 **A:** Shall I cook something?
  B: That sounds like a good idea. I'm hungry.
2 **A:** Let's go to a football match.
  B: Yes, OK then. We all love sport.
3 **A:** Why don't we phone and book tickets?
  B: No, let's get the tickets online. We can save money.
4 **A:** How about going to the music festival this weekend?
  B: OK. My favourite band is playing on Saturday.
5 **A:** I'll ask Sarah to come.
  B: Good idea. Have you got her phone number?
6 **A:** Why don't you make some coffee?
  B: No! I made it last time! Why don't you make it?

UNIT 12 RECORDING 7

D: Dad   **A:** Anna   **N:** Nick   **M:** Mum
D: Well, everybody, what shall we do today? Any ideas?
A: I'm not sure – it depends on the weather. Is it sunny outside?
D: Just a minute . . . No, not exactly. In fact, it's raining again!
N: Why don't we stay here? We can play computer games.
M: I know what we can do. Let's have a look at the guidebook. I'm sure we can find some ideas in there.
D: That sounds like a good idea. Well, there's the Museum of Country Life – how about that?
N: Hmm . . . is there anything more exciting?
D: Well, why don't we go to Aqua World?
N: Yes, that sounds better. Shall we go there?
A: All right. It'll be fun.
M: Shall we book tickets online? It's probably cheaper.
D: Good idea. So, everyone's happy!

UNIT 13 RECORDING 1

1 A: Does Bruce have to look after the passengers?
   B: Yes, he does.
2 A: Does he have to use a computer?
   B: No, he doesn't.
3 A: Does he have to look smart?
   B: Yes, he does.
4 A: Does George have to fly the plane?
   B: Yes, he does.
5 A: Does he have to serve food?
   B: No, he doesn't.
6 A: Does he have to wear a uniform?
   B: Yes, he does.
7 A: Do Alizia and Meera have to wear a uniform?
   B: No, they don't.
8 A: Do they have to travel a lot?
   B: No, they don't.

UNIT 13 RECORDING 4

1 We might go swimming this afternoon.
2 The plane might arrive late.
3 You might be rich one day if you work hard.
4 I might not be able to come to class next week.
5 I might not see Frank this weekend.
6 Philip might not stay until the end of the course.
7 The government might change soon.
8 The exam might not be as difficult as you think.

UNIT 14 RECORDING 1

1	sleep	slept
2	make	made
3	lose	lost
4	stand	stood
5	speak	spoken
6	take	taken
7	drive	driven
8	write	written
9	say	said
10	come	come
11	give	given
12	keep	kept
13	tell	told
14	become	become
15	see	seen

UNIT 14 RECORDING 2

1 A: Has Richard always lived in Hexham?
   B: Yes, he has.
2 A: Has Elaine ever lived in another town?
   B: Yes, she has.
3 A: Have they always lived in the same house?
   B: No, they haven't.
4 A: Has Gordon always been a teacher?
   B: No, he hasn't.
5 A: Has he ever worked abroad?
   B: Yes, he has.
6 A: Have Gordon and Sarah always lived in Leeds?
   B: No, they haven't.
7 A: Has Sarah had her own business before?
   B: No, she hasn't.
8 A: Has Rebecca left school?
   B: Yes, she has.

UNIT 14 RECORDING 4

1 A: Mum, have I ever done anything really bad?
   B: Yes, you have! When you were about two years old, you were very naughty!
2 A: Have you ever bought a painting from an artist?
   B: No, I haven't. I'm not really very interested in art.
3 A: Has there ever been a female Prime Minister in the United Kingdom?
   B: Yes, there has. Margaret Thatcher in the 1980s.
4 A: Have you ever met a famous person?
   B: No, I haven't. I saw Robbie Williams in concert, but I didn't speak to him!
5 A: Has your computer ever had a virus?
   B: No, it hasn't. I've got ant-virus software on it.
6 A: Have you ever visited Ireland?
   B: Yes, I have. I went to Dublin last year and I had a great time.

UNIT 14 RECORDING 5

1 A: Have you ever been in love?
   B: Yes, I have. It was when I was 16.
2 A: Have you ever lost your wallet?
   B: No, I've never lost my wallet, but I have found some money on the street.
3 A: Have your mum and dad ever travelled by plane?
   B: Yes, they have. They've flown to the USA twice.
4 A: Has it ever snowed in Saudi Arabia?
   B: No, it hasn't.

Pearson Education Limited
Edinburgh Gate
Harlow
Essex CM20 2JE
England
and Associated Companies throughout the world.

www.pearsonelt.com

First published 2013
Fifth impression 2016

ISBN: 978-1-4479-0640-7

Set in 10.5pt Bliss Light
Printed in Malaysia, PJB - CTP

Photo acknowledgements
*The publisher would like to thank the following for their kind permission
to reproduce their photographs:*

(Key: b-bottom; c-centre; l-left; r-right; t-top)

Alamy Images: Huntstock, Inc 6cr, studiomode 9/13; **Bridgeman Art
Library Ltd:** Private Collection / Ken Welsh 34t, Universal History
Archive / UIG 42tr; Corbis: Ben Queenborough / BPI 5c, Bettmann 34,
35t, Danny Moloshok / Reuters 72l, Hulton-Deutsch Collection 42bl,
Imaginechina 72br, Manish Paudel / Demotix 31l; **FLPA Images of
Nature:** Kevin Elsby 55tr; **Fotolia.com:** Aaron Amat 9/14, anankkml
32, Yuri Arcurs 4tr, bloomua 9/6, paul_brighton 33, determined 9/11,
Jaimie Duplass 20r, Elnur 9/1, full image 9/4, kavring 9/8, Vasiliy
Koval 55br, Bernd Libbach 46tr, Monkey Business 17, Linda More 57b,
okinawakasawa 9/15, paultarasenko 6tl, pio3 13, Sergejs Rahunoks 4l,
Sergey Peterman 9/9, Silkstock 9/10, Wrangler 51bl; **Getty Images:**
Cover 12, Globo 35b; **Mary Evans Picture Library:** SZ Photo / Scherl
34c; **MIXA Co Ltd:** 4br; **Pearson Education Ltd:** Coleman Yuen
9/7; **Photoshot Holdings Limited:** AdMedia 72tr, NHPA 55tl; **Press
Association Images:** M. Spencer Green / AP 5r, Winfried Rothermel /
AP 72cr; **Reuters:** Jo Yong Hak 18; **Rex Features:** 5l, Stuart Clarke /
Associated Newspapers 37; **Shutterstock.com:** artjazz 9/3, Jose AS
Reyes 51tl, Andre Blais 71t, Goran Bogicevic 45, Zdenka Darula
53, Dragon Images 8, Jaimie Duplass 6tr, Fotoluminate LLC 6bl,
Glovatskiy 51cr, hainaultphoto 57t, Oliver Hoffmann 9/12, iofoto 6cl,
JNT Visual 9/2, jocic 9/5, Lee Kennedy 22, Philip Lange 30, Monkey
Business Images 71c, oliveromg 71b, Phase4Photography 4cr, Standret
9/16

Cover images: *Front:* **Fotolia.com:** Kushnirov Avraham

All other images © Pearson Education

Every effort has been made to trace the copyright holders and we
apologise in advance for any unintentional omissions. We would be
pleased to insert the appropriate acknowledgement in any subsequent
edition of this publication.

Illustrated by Jeff Anderson, Gary Andrews, Kes Hankin (Gemini
Design), Conny Jude, Chris Pavely, Theresa Tibbetts (Beehive
Illustration), Mark Vallance (Gemini Design) and Moreno Chiacchiera
(Beehive Illustration).